NICE 3-DAY TRAVE

Welcome to Nice, the vibrant and cosmopolitan city nestled on the sparkling shores of the French Riviera. With its sunny weather, stunning seafront, and rich history and culture, Nice has something to offer every traveler.

Whether you're strolling along the famous Promenade des Anglais, exploring the charming Old Town (Vieux Nice), or taking in the panoramic views from Castle Hill (Colline du Château), you'll be enchanted by the city's beauty and charm.

In this travel guide, we'll take you on a journey through the top attractions in Nice, from its historic landmarks to its world-class museums and galleries. We'll also introduce you to the city's vibrant food and drink scene, with its tempting array of local specialties and international cuisines, as well as its lively bars and nightlife.

If you're in the mood for some shopping, we'll show you where to find the best boutiques, markets, and souvenirs in Nice, while also highlighting some of the city's nearby excursions to other beautiful spots on the French Riviera.

To help you make the most of your visit to Nice, we'll also provide practical information on accommodation options, money and tipping, language, safety, health, and local customs and etiquette.

So whether you're a first-time visitor or a seasoned traveler, we hope this travel guide will inspire you to discover all that Nice has to offer and make your visit an unforgettable experience.

Contents

I. Introduction

About Nice

Located on the southeast coast of France, Nice is the fifth largest city in the country and the second most popular tourist destination after Paris. It's situated on the sparkling waters of the Mediterranean Sea and is surrounded by the beautiful hills of the Alpes-Maritimes region.

Nice has a rich history dating back to the ancient Greeks, who founded the city in the 4th century BC. Over the centuries, it has been ruled by various powers, including the Romans, the Moors, and the House of Savoy, before finally becoming part of France in 1860.

Today, Nice is a vibrant and cosmopolitan city that attracts visitors from around the world with its warm climate, stunning beaches, and unique blend of French and Mediterranean culture. It's also known for its beautiful architecture, art museums, and cuisine, including the famous Nicoise salad, socca (a type of chickpea pancake), and local seafood dishes.

One of the city's most iconic landmarks is the Promenade des Anglais, a picturesque walkway that runs along the coastline for several kilometers. The Old Town (Vieux Nice) is another popular destination, with its narrow streets, colorful buildings, and lively markets.

Nice is also an important transportation hub, with a major international airport and a train station that connects it to other cities in France and Europe. This makes it an ideal base for exploring the rest of the French Riviera, including nearby towns like Cannes, Antibes, and Monaco.

Whether you're interested in history, art, food, or simply soaking up the sun and sea, Nice has something to offer every traveler. So come and discover this beautiful and vibrant city for yourself!

Why Visit Nice

There are countless reasons to visit Nice, one of the most beautiful and vibrant cities on the French Riviera. Here are just a few:

- Stunning beaches: Nice is famous for its beautiful beaches, including the Promenade des Anglais, which stretches for several kilometers along the Mediterranean Sea. Whether you want to swim, sunbathe, or simply relax with a book, there's a beach in Nice that's perfect for you.
- Fascinating history and culture: With a history that dates back to ancient Greece, Nice is a city with a rich cultural heritage. From its historic landmarks and museums to its lively markets and festivals, there's always something new to discover in this vibrant and cosmopolitan city.
- Delicious cuisine: If you're a foodie, you'll love the cuisine in Nice, which combines the best of French and Mediterranean flavors. From local specialties like socca and Nicoise salad to international cuisine from around the world, there's something to please every palate.
- Beautiful architecture: Nice is home to some of the most beautiful architecture in France, including the colorful buildings of the Old Town (Vieux Nice) and the grand Belle Epoque mansions that line the Promenade des Anglais. Whether you're an architecture buff or simply appreciate beautiful buildings, you'll be enchanted by the city's unique and diverse architecture.

- Proximity to other attractions: Nice is located in the heart of the French Riviera, making it an ideal base for exploring nearby towns and attractions like Cannes, Antibes, Monaco, and Saint-Tropez. Whether you're interested in art, history, or simply soaking up the sun and sea, there's plenty to see and do in the surrounding area.

So whether you're looking for a relaxing beach vacation, a cultural adventure, or simply a chance to explore one of the most beautiful regions in France, Nice is the perfect destination. Come and discover all that this vibrant and cosmopolitan city has to offer!

When to Visit Nice

Nice is a year-round destination, with a mild Mediterranean climate that makes it a pleasant place to visit at any time of the year. However, the best time to visit depends on your preferences and interests.

If you're looking for warm weather and plenty of sunshine, the summer months of June, July, and August are the most popular. During this time, temperatures can reach up to 30°C (86°F), and the beaches and restaurants are crowded with tourists. However, it's also the driest time of the year, with only a few days of rain each month.

If you prefer milder temperatures and smaller crowds, the shoulder seasons of May, September, and October are a good choice. During these months, the weather is still warm and sunny, with temperatures averaging around 20-25°C (68-77°F). There are also fewer tourists, so you'll have a better chance of finding accommodation and enjoying the city's attractions without the crowds.

Winter is the low season in Nice, but it's still a good time to visit if you're interested in cultural attractions or winter sports. December, January, and February are the coldest months, with temperatures ranging from 5-15°C (41-59°F). There are also more rainy days during this time, but the city is still lively with Christmas markets and other holiday events.

Here is a bulleted list with each month's weather in Nice:

- March: Low 9°C (48°F), High 15°C (59°F), 7 rainy days
- April: Low 11°C (52°F), High 18°C (64°F), 7 rainy days
- May: Low 14°C (57°F), High 22°C (72°F), 6 rainy days
- June: Low 18°C (64°F), High 26°C (79°F), 3 rainy days
- July: Low 21°C (70°F), High 29°C (84°F), 1 rainy day
- August: Low 21°C (70°F), High 29°C (84°F), 1 rainy day
- September: Low 18°C (64°F), High 25°C (77°F), 4 rainy days
- October: Low 14°C (57°F), High 21°C (70°F), 8 rainy days
- November: Low 11°C (52°F), High 17°C (63°F), 8 rainy days
- December: Low 7°C (45°F), High 13°C (55°F), 8 rainy days
- January: Low 6°C (43°F), High 13°C (55°F), 9 rainy days
- February: Low 7°C (45°F), High 14°C (57°F), 8 rainy days

No matter when you visit Nice, there's always something to see and do. Just be sure to pack accordingly for the weather and plan your itinerary accordingly!

Getting to Nice

Nice is a major transportation hub, with several options for getting to the city from other parts of France and Europe.

By Plane:

Nice Côte d'Azur International Airport is located just a few kilometers from the city center and is served by numerous airlines from around the world. There are direct flights from major cities in Europe, as well as direct flights from North America and Asia. Once you arrive at the airport, you can take a taxi or bus to the city center.

By Train:

Nice is connected to other cities in France and Europe by the TGV (high-speed train) and regional trains. The main train station, Nice-Ville, is located in the city center and is served by trains from Paris, Marseille, Cannes, and other cities. There are also international trains from Milan, Genoa, and other Italian cities that stop in Nice.

By Car:

If you're driving to Nice, the city is easily accessible from other parts of France and Europe via the A8 motorway. However, be aware that traffic can be heavy, especially during the summer months, and parking can be expensive and difficult to find in the city center.

By Bus:

Several bus companies operate routes to Nice from other cities in France and Europe, including Eurolines, Flixbus, and Ouibus. Most buses arrive at the central bus station, located on Avenue Thiers in the city center.

By Boat:

If you're coming from other parts of the Mediterranean, there are ferry services that connect Nice to Corsica, Sardinia, and other nearby islands. The main ferry port is located in the city center, near the Promenade des Anglais.

No matter how you choose to get to Nice, be sure to book your travel in advance to get the best prices and avoid any last-minute complications.

Getting Around Nice

Nice is a compact and walkable city, but if you want to explore further afield or don't feel like walking, there are several other transportation options available.

Public Transportation:

The public transportation system in Nice is operated by Lignes d'Azur and includes buses and trams. The tram system runs from the northern suburbs to the city center, while the buses cover the entire city and surrounding areas. Tickets can be purchased at kiosks, vending machines, or on board the bus or tram, and cost €1.50 for a one-way trip or €10 for a 10-trip pass.

Taxis:

Taxis are readily available in Nice, but they can be expensive, especially during peak tourist season. Taxis in Nice are required to use a meter, but be sure to confirm the price with the driver before getting in. If you prefer to use a taxi app, Uber and Bolt are available in Nice.

Here are some sample prices for taxis in Nice:

- Nice Airport to city center: €32-35
- City center to Promenade des Anglais: €10-15
- City center to Old Town: €10-15

Bicycle Rentals:

Bicycles are a great way to explore Nice, and there are several rental companies in the city, including Vélo Bleu and Blue Bike. Both companies offer rental rates starting at €1 per hour or €5 per day, and have stations throughout the city where you can pick up and drop off bikes.

Walking:

One of the best ways to explore Nice is on foot. The city center is compact and easy to navigate, and there are several pedestrian-only streets and pathways. Walking is also a great way to discover hidden gems and take in the city's unique charm.

No matter how you choose to get around Nice, be sure to plan your routes in advance and allow extra time for traffic and crowds during peak tourist season. If you're using a taxi app, be sure to have a working data plan or access to Wi-Fi to avoid roaming charges.

Nice Tourist Pass

The **Nice Tourist Pass**, also known as the **French Riviera Pass**, is an all-inclusive card that offers visitors access to a variety of top attractions, museums, and activities in Nice and the surrounding region. It's an excellent way to save money and enjoy a hassle-free vacation while exploring the French Riviera.

There are three different pass options available:

1. 24-hour pass: €26
2. 48-hour pass: €38
3. 72-hour pass: €56

With the Nice Tourist Pass, you'll gain free entry to more than *50 attractions and museums* in Nice and the French Riviera, including:

- Musée Matisse
- Musée Marc Chagall
- Musée d'Art Moderne et d'Art Contemporain (MAMAC)

- Villa Ephrussi de Rothschild
- Monaco Oceanographic Museum

In addition to free entry, the pass also offers various discounts on activities such as guided tours, bike rentals, and boat trips. You can also benefit from *unlimited free access to public transportation* within Nice, making it easy to get around and explore the city.

To make the most of your Nice Tourist Pass, plan your itinerary in advance and prioritize the attractions and activities that interest you the most. Keep in mind that some attractions may have limited hours or require advance booking, so be sure to check their websites for the latest information.

The Nice Tourist Pass can be purchased *online* at the official website (www.frenchrivierapass.com) or at the *Nice Tourism Office*, located at 5 Promenade des Anglais, 06000 Nice. Once you've purchased the pass, you'll need to activate it by writing your name and the date of first use on the back. The pass will be valid for 24, 48, or 72 hours from the time of activation, depending on the option you've chosen. For more information and a complete list of attractions included in the Nice Tourist Pass, visit the official website: www.frenchrivierapass.com.

II. Top Attractions

Nice is a city full of beautiful and fascinating attractions, from its historic landmarks and museums to its stunning beaches and parks. Whether you're interested in art, history, or simply soaking up the sun and sea, there's something to suit every taste in this vibrant and cosmopolitan city.

In this section, we'll introduce you to some of the top attractions in Nice, including its famous Promenade des Anglais, charming Old Town (Vieux Nice), and panoramic views from Castle Hill (Colline du Château). We'll also take you on a journey through the city's world-class museums and galleries, including the Musée Matisse, Musée Marc Chagall, and Musée d'Art Moderne et d'Art Contemporain (MAMAC).

Whether you're a first-time visitor or a seasoned traveler, we hope this section will inspire you to discover the best that Nice has to offer and make your visit an unforgettable experience. So let's dive in and explore the top attractions in this beautiful and vibrant city!

Promenade des Anglais

One of the most iconic landmarks in Nice, the Promenade des Anglais is a stunning seaside walkway that runs along the Baie des Anges (Bay of Angels) for several kilometers. The promenade was first built in the 18th century by English aristocrats who visited Nice for its mild climate and stunning scenery. Today, it's a popular destination for locals and tourists alike, who come to stroll, cycle, or simply relax on the beach and take in the beautiful views of the Mediterranean Sea.

The promenade is lined with grand Belle Epoque hotels, including the legendary Negresco Hotel, as well as palm trees, gardens, and fountains. There are also several public and private beaches along the promenade, where you can rent chairs and umbrellas or enjoy water sports like jet skiing and parasailing.

At the eastern end of the promenade, you'll find the famous "Angel's Bay" statue, which overlooks the sea and the city. The statue, which was created in 1950 by the French artist, Maurice Calka, has become an iconic symbol of Nice and is a popular spot for taking photos.

Whether you're in the mood for a leisurely stroll, a bike ride, or simply soaking up the sun and sea, the Promenade des Anglais is a must-see attraction in Nice. So grab your sunglasses and sunscreen, and come and discover this beautiful seaside walkway for yourself!

Old Town (Vieux Nice)

The Old Town, or Vieux Nice, is one of the most charming and picturesque parts of Nice. Located in the heart of the city, it's a maze of narrow streets, colorful buildings, and lively markets that date back to the Middle Ages.

Wandering through the Old Town, you'll discover hidden squares, historic churches, and quaint cafes that serve up local specialties like socca (a type of chickpea pancake) and pan bagnat (a Nicoise sandwich made with tuna and vegetables). You'll also find plenty of artisan shops selling handmade crafts and souvenirs, as well as art galleries and boutique stores.

One of the main attractions in the Old Town is the Cours Saleya market, which is held every day except Monday. Here, you'll find a colorful array of fresh produce, flowers, and artisanal products. On Mondays, the market is transformed into an antique market, where you can browse for unique and vintage items.

The Old Town is also home to several historic landmarks, including the Cathédrale Sainte-Réparate, a beautiful baroque church that dates back to the 17th century, and the Palais Lascaris, a grand 17th-century mansion that now houses a museum of musical instruments.

One of the best ways to explore the Old Town is on foot, as many of the streets are too narrow for cars. Be sure to wear comfortable shoes and allow plenty of time to get lost in the labyrinthine streets and discover the hidden gems of this charming and historic neighborhood.

Overall, the Old Town is a must-see attraction in Nice, full of history, culture, and local charm. So come and discover the magic of Vieux Nice for yourself!

Castle Hill (Colline du Château)

Perched high above the city, Castle Hill (Colline du Château) is one of the most popular and picturesque attractions in Nice. The hill is a natural park that offers panoramic views of the city, the sea, and the surrounding hills. It's a great place to take a walk, have a picnic, or simply soak up the stunning views.

Castle Hill gets its name from the ruined castle that once stood at the top of the hill. The castle was built in the 11th century by the Counts of Provence and was a strategic military fortress for several centuries. Today, only a few ruins remain, but they are still a popular attraction for visitors.

To reach the top of Castle Hill, you can take the stairs, which start at the eastern end of the Promenade des Anglais, or the elevator, which is located near the port. Once you reach the top, you'll be rewarded with breathtaking views of the city and the sea. You'll also find several other attractions, including a waterfall, a playground, and a cafe.

One of the best times to visit Castle Hill is at sunset, when the sky is painted with shades of orange, pink, and purple. The views from the top are truly spectacular, and it's a romantic and magical spot to watch the sun go down.

Nice Cathedral (Cathédrale Sainte-Réparate)

Located in the heart of the Old Town, Nice Cathedral, also known as Cathédrale Sainte-Réparate, is a beautiful baroque church that dates back to the 17th century. The cathedral is dedicated to Saint Reparata, a young girl who was martyred in the 3rd century and is the patron saint of Nice.

The cathedral's exterior features a beautiful pink and white facade with intricate carvings and statues. The interior is equally stunning, with a high altar made of Italian marble, beautiful stained glass windows, and an ornate organ. The cathedral also houses several chapels, each dedicated to a different saint.

One of the most impressive features of the cathedral is the collection of religious artwork, including paintings and sculptures by renowned artists such as Louis Brea and Ludovico Brea. The cathedral's treasury also contains several priceless religious artifacts, including a reliquary that allegedly contains the bones of Saint Reparata.

The cathedral is open to visitors every day, except during religious services. Admission is free, but donations are appreciated. If you're interested in learning more about the cathedral and its history, guided tours are available in several languages.

Overall, Nice Cathedral is a beautiful and historic attraction that is well worth a visit when you're in the Old Town. Whether you're interested in art, history, or religion, you'll find plenty to appreciate in this stunning baroque church.

Place Masséna

Located in the heart of the city, Place Masséna is one of the most vibrant and lively squares in Nice. It was named after André Masséna, a French general who was born in Nice and served under Napoleon Bonaparte.

The square is a pedestrian zone and is surrounded by grand buildings with colorful facades and elaborate balconies. It's also home to several impressive works of art, including a series of seven statues, called "Conversation in Nice," that depict men and women in animated discussion.

One of the most striking features of the square is the massive black-and-white checkerboard pavement, which was designed by the Spanish artist, Jaume Plensa. The pavement features a series of water jets that shoot up intermittently, creating a playful and interactive atmosphere.

Place Masséna is also a popular destination for shopping and dining. The square is surrounded by several cafes, restaurants, and boutique shops, where you can find everything from local specialties to high-end designer brands. The Galeries Lafayette department store, which is housed in a grand Art Nouveau building, is also located nearby.

Throughout the year, Place Masséna hosts several events and festivals, including the annual Nice Carnival, which is one of the largest and most colorful carnivals in the world. During the carnival, the square is transformed into a massive party, with parades, music, and fireworks.

Overall, Place Masséna is a must-see attraction in Nice, full of energy, art, and culture. Whether you're looking to shop, dine, or simply soak up the atmosphere, you'll find plenty to enjoy in this vibrant and lively square.

Cours Saleya Flower Market

Located in the heart of the Old Town, Cours Saleya Flower Market is a colorful and fragrant market that is a must-visit attraction in Nice. The market is held every day except Monday and is one of the oldest and most famous markets in the city.

The market is a feast for the senses, with rows of vendors selling flowers, fruits, vegetables, and local specialties. The flower market is the star of the show, with a stunning array of fresh blooms in every color of the rainbow. From delicate roses to exotic orchids, there's something for every taste and budget.

In addition to flowers, the market also sells a variety of locally grown fruits and vegetables, including tomatoes, olives, and lemons. You'll also find artisanal products like honey, jam, and olive oil, as well as handicrafts and souvenirs.

The market is a popular destination for locals and tourists alike, and the atmosphere is lively and vibrant. Be sure to take your time and soak up the sights and smells of this unique and colorful market.

In the evening, the market transforms into a bustling restaurant scene, with outdoor seating and live music. It's a great place to relax and enjoy a glass of wine and some local cuisine.

Overall, Cours Saleya Flower Market is a must-visit attraction in Nice, full of local color and culture. Whether you're looking to buy flowers, taste local specialties, or simply people-watch, you'll find plenty to enjoy in this lively and vibrant market.

Musée Matisse

The Musée Matisse is a world-class museum dedicated to the life and works of the famous French artist, Henri Matisse. The museum is located in the Cimiez neighborhood of Nice, in a beautiful 17th-century villa that was once the home of Matisse.

The museum's collection includes more than 400 paintings, sculptures, drawings, and prints by Matisse, as well as several of his personal belongings, including photographs, letters, and souvenirs. The collection spans Matisse's entire career, from his early works to his famous cut-outs.

Here are the 10 best exhibits to see at Musée Matisse:

1. "The Joy of Life" (Le Bonheur de Vivre) - a masterpiece of Fauvism that depicts a group of nudes in a lush, colorful landscape.
2. "Blue Nude" (Nu Bleu) - a series of paintings and drawings that feature Matisse's signature blue color.
3. "The Dance" (La Danse) - a large painting that depicts a group of dancers in motion.
4. "The Moroccan Paintings" - a series of works that were inspired by Matisse's travels to Morocco in the early 1900s.

5. "The Cut-Outs" - a series of works that Matisse created by cutting and pasting paper into abstract shapes.
6. "Odalisques" - a series of paintings that feature reclining female figures in exotic costumes.
7. "Interior with Goldfish" (Intérieur aux poissons rouges) - a painting that features a goldfish bowl as the focal point.
8. "The Still Lifes" - a series of works that feature everyday objects like fruit, flowers, and vases.
9. "The Nice Period" - a series of works that Matisse created during his time living in Nice.
10. "Matisse's Studio" - an exhibit that recreates Matisse's studio, including his furniture, books, and art supplies.

The museum is open every day except Tuesday, from 10 am to 6 pm. Admission is €10 for adults and free for children under 18. Audio guides are available in several languages for an additional fee.

The museum is easily accessible by public transportation, with several bus stops and a tram stop nearby. There is also a large parking lot nearby for visitors who are driving.

Overall, the Musée Matisse is a must-visit attraction in Nice for art lovers and anyone interested in the life and works of one of the most influential artists of the 20th century. So be sure to add it to your itinerary when you visit this beautiful city!

Musée Marc Chagall

The Musée Marc Chagall is a stunning museum dedicated to the life and works of the famous Russian-born artist, Marc Chagall. The museum is located in the Cimiez neighborhood of Nice, in a beautiful modernist building surrounded by a peaceful garden.

The museum's collection includes over 400 works by Chagall, including paintings, sculptures, ceramics, and tapestries. The collection spans Chagall's entire career, from his early works to his later masterpieces.

Here are the 10 best exhibits to see at Musée Marc Chagall:

1. "The Biblical Message" - a series of 17 large-scale paintings that depict scenes from the Old and New Testaments.
2. "The Song of Songs" - a series of paintings and drawings that illustrate passages from the Song of Songs in the Bible.
3. "The Fourteen Stations of the Cross" - a series of paintings that depict the Stations of the Cross.
4. "The Ceiling of the Paris Opera" - a stunning ceiling mural that Chagall created for the Paris Opera in 1964.
5. "The Paris Windows" - a series of stained-glass windows that Chagall created for the Saint-Paul-de-Vence chapel.
6. "The Daphnis and Chloe Series" - a series of lithographs that Chagall created for a special edition of the ancient Greek novel Daphnis and Chloe.
7. "The Russian Period" - a series of paintings and sketches that Chagall created during his time living in Russia.
8. "The Nice Period" - a series of works that Chagall created during his time living in Nice.
9. "The War Years" - a series of paintings that Chagall created during World War II.
10. "The Later Works" - a series of works that Chagall created in his later years, including several large-scale murals.

The museum is open every day except Tuesday, from 10 am to 5 pm (closed on certain holidays). Admission is €10 for adults and free for children under 18. Audio guides are available in several languages for an additional fee.

The museum is easily accessible by public transportation, with several bus stops and a tram stop nearby. There is also a large parking lot nearby for visitors who are driving.

Overall, the Musée Marc Chagall is a must-visit attraction in Nice for art lovers and anyone interested in the life and works of one of the most influential artists of the 20th century. So be sure to add it to your itinerary when you visit this beautiful city!

Musée d'Art Moderne et d'Art Contemporain (MAMAC)

The Musée d'Art Moderne et d'Art Contemporain (MAMAC) is a must-visit museum for modern and contemporary art lovers. The museum is located in the heart of Nice, in a striking building that was designed by the architect Yves Bayard.

The museum's collection includes over 1,300 works of art, including paintings, sculptures, photographs, videos, and installations. The collection focuses on art from the 20th and 21st centuries and includes works by some of the most important artists of the era.

Here are the 10 best exhibits to see at Musée d'Art Moderne et d'Art Contemporain (MAMAC):

1. "The School of Nice" - an exhibit that features works by a group of artists who were associated with the art movement known as the School of Nice.
2. "Pop Art" - an exhibit that features works by some of the most important artists of the Pop Art movement, including Andy Warhol and Roy Lichtenstein.

3. "Minimalism" - an exhibit that features works by artists associated with the Minimalist movement, including Dan Flavin and Donald Judd.
4. "Street Art" - an exhibit that features works by some of the most important street artists of the past few decades, including Banksy and Shepard Fairey.
5. "Photography" - an exhibit that features works by some of the most important photographers of the 20th and 21st centuries, including Man Ray and Cindy Sherman.
6. "Abstraction" - an exhibit that features works by artists associated with the Abstract Expressionist movement, including Jackson Pollock and Mark Rothko.
7. "The CoBrA Group" - an exhibit that features works by artists who were associated with the CoBrA Group, an art movement that was active in the 1940s and 1950s.
8. "The Fluxus Movement" - an exhibit that features works by artists who were associated with the Fluxus movement, an avant-garde art movement that was active in the 1960s and 1970s.
9. "The New Realists" - an exhibit that features works by artists associated with the New Realism movement, including Yves Klein and Arman.
10. "Contemporary Art" - an exhibit that features works by some of the most important contemporary artists of the past few decades, including Damien Hirst and Jeff Koons.

The museum is open every day except Tuesday, from 10 am to 6 pm. Admission is €10 for adults and free for children under 18. Audio guides are available in several languages for an additional fee.

The museum is easily accessible by public transportation, with several bus stops and a tram stop nearby. There is also a large parking lot nearby for visitors who are driving.

Overall, the Musée d'Art Moderne et d'Art Contemporain (MAMAC) is a must-visit attraction in Nice for art lovers and anyone interested in the most important art movements of the past century.

Phoenix Park (Parc Phoenix)

Phoenix Park, also known as Parc Phoenix, is a beautiful green oasis located near the airport in Nice. The park covers over 7 hectares and is home to over 2,500 species of plants, as well as several animal exhibits.

The park is a great destination for families, nature lovers, and anyone looking for a peaceful escape from the city. It features several walking paths, ponds, and gardens, as well as several children's play areas.

One of the park's main attractions is the large greenhouse, which is one of the largest in Europe. The greenhouse is divided into several sections, each featuring a different type of vegetation, from tropical rainforests to arid deserts. Visitors can also see several species of birds and butterflies that call the greenhouse home.

The park is also home to several animal exhibits, including a reptile house, an insectarium, and a farm. Visitors can see everything from turtles and snakes to pigs and sheep. The park also hosts several daily animal shows, including a bird of prey demonstration.

In addition to its natural and animal exhibits, Phoenix Park also hosts several cultural events throughout the year, including art exhibitions, concerts, and festivals.

Overall, Phoenix Park is a great destination for anyone looking to escape the hustle and bustle of the city and enjoy a peaceful and beautiful natural setting. So be sure to add it to your itinerary when you visit Nice!

Russian Orthodox Cathedral (Cathédrale Orthodoxe Russe Saint-Nicolas)

The *Russian Orthodox Cathedral*, also known as the *Cathédrale Orthodoxe Russe Saint-Nicolas*, is a stunning architectural gem and an important religious site located in Nice. Built in 1912, it is considered one of the most beautiful Russian Orthodox churches outside of Russia and a must-visit attraction for anyone interested in history, architecture, or religion.

The cathedral was built to serve the growing Russian community in Nice, which included the Russian aristocracy who visited the French Riviera during the late 19th and early 20th centuries. The cathedral is dedicated to *Saint Nicholas*, the patron saint of Russia, and its construction was financed by Tsar Nicholas II.

The cathedral's architecture is a striking example of *neo-Byzantine style*, characterized by its ornate domes, vibrant colors, and intricate details. The exterior features six onion-shaped domes, with the central and largest dome symbolizing Jesus Christ and the smaller ones representing the four evangelists and the Virgin Mary. The façade is adorned with beautiful mosaics and religious icons, which contribute to the cathedral's impressive appearance.

Inside the cathedral, visitors will find a richly decorated interior with a wealth of religious art, including frescoes, icons, and wood carvings. Among the most notable pieces is a beautiful iconostasis, a traditional screen that separates the sanctuary from the nave, adorned with icons depicting scenes from the life of Christ and various saints.

Visiting the Russian Orthodox Cathedral

The Russian Orthodox Cathedral is located at *Avenue Nicolas II, 06000 Nice*. It is easily accessible by public transportation, with the nearest tram stop, *Alsace-Lorraine*, just a 5-minute walk away.

Opening hours:

- Tuesday to Sunday: 9:00 AM – 12:00 PM and 2:00 PM – 6:00 PM
- Closed on Mondays and during religious services

Admission: Free entry, but donations are welcome.

Guided tours are available upon request, and it's recommended to contact the cathedral in advance to arrange a tour. Keep in mind that this is an active place of worship, so visitors are expected to dress modestly and be respectful of the religious practices taking place.

For more information about the Russian Orthodox Cathedral, visit their official website: www.acor-nice.com.

III. Food and Drink

No visit to Nice would be complete without experiencing the city's famous cuisine. Nice's culinary scene is as diverse as it is delicious, with a mix of Mediterranean and French influences that make for a truly unique dining experience. From traditional Provençal dishes to fresh seafood, there's something for every taste and budget.

In addition to its food, Nice is also famous for its wine. The city is located in the heart of the Côte d'Azur wine region, which produces some of the finest wines in France. Whether you're a wine connoisseur or simply looking to enjoy a glass with your meal, Nice has plenty to offer.

In this section, we'll explore the best restaurants, cafés, bars, and markets that Nice has to offer. We'll also provide tips on the best local dishes to try, as well as where to find the best wines and other drinks. So get ready to indulge in the flavors of Nice!

Typical Niçoise Cuisine

Niçoise cuisine is a delicious blend of French and Mediterranean flavors, with an emphasis on fresh, locally sourced ingredients. The cuisine is heavily influenced by the region's coastal location, with a focus on seafood and vegetables.

Here are some of the most typical Niçoise dishes you should try:

1. Salade Niçoise - a fresh salad made with tomatoes, lettuce, hard-boiled eggs, anchovies, and tuna.
2. Socca - a crispy pancake made with chickpea flour and olive oil.
3. Pissaladière - a savory tart made with caramelized onions, anchovies, and olives.
4. Ratatouille - a vegetable stew made with eggplant, zucchini, peppers, and tomatoes.

5. Farcis Niçois - vegetables like tomatoes, zucchini, and eggplant are stuffed with a meat and vegetable mixture and baked.
6. Bouillabaisse - a classic seafood stew made with a variety of fish, shellfish, and vegetables.
7. Pan bagnat - a sandwich made with tuna, hard-boiled eggs, tomatoes, and olives on a crusty roll.

When it comes to dessert, be sure to try the local specialties:

1. Pissalat - a sweet bread made with olive oil and orange blossom water.
2. Tourte de Blettes - a sweet tart made with Swiss chard, pine nuts, and raisins.
3. Farcis sucrés - a sweet dessert made with fruits like figs or peaches that are stuffed with a mixture of breadcrumbs, sugar, and almonds.

To enjoy the local cuisine to the fullest, visit the city's many markets, where you can find fresh produce, seafood, and other local specialties. Some of the best markets in Nice include the Cours Saleya Market and the Liberation Market.

In terms of drinks, wine is the most popular beverage in Nice. Local wines from the surrounding vineyards include the Bellet and Côtes de Provence appellations. Local beers and spirits are also available, as well as the famous pastis, an anise-flavored aperitif that is popular in the region.

Overall, the Niçoise cuisine is a must-try when visiting Nice. So be sure to sample as many local dishes as possible during your stay!

Restaurants and Cafes

Nice's culinary scene is as diverse as it is delicious, with a mix of traditional French and Mediterranean flavors that make for a truly unique dining experience. The city is home to a wide range of restaurants and cafes, from cozy bistros to upscale fine dining establishments.

Here are some of the best restaurants and cafes in Nice:

1. La Petite Maison - a popular fine dining restaurant that serves traditional Niçoise cuisine, such as stuffed vegetables and fish dishes. Reservations are highly recommended.
2. Chez Palmyre - a family-run bistro that has been serving traditional Niçoise dishes for over 90 years. Be sure to try their socca and pissaladière.
3. Lou Pistou - a cozy restaurant that serves classic French cuisine with a Mediterranean twist. Their fish dishes and seafood platters are a must-try.
4. La Zucca Magica - a vegetarian restaurant that offers a unique and creative menu featuring local and organic ingredients. Reservations are recommended.
5. Les Amoureux - a charming bistro that serves traditional French cuisine in a cozy and romantic setting. Their escargots and duck confit are highly recommended.
6. Café de Turin - a historic café that has been serving fresh seafood and shellfish for over a century. Be sure to try their oysters and mussels.
7. La Cave de la Tour - a wine bar that serves a wide selection of local wines and small plates of charcuterie and cheese.
8. Café Marché - a cozy cafe that serves breakfast, lunch, and brunch featuring fresh and locally sourced ingredients.

9. La Favola - a casual Italian restaurant that serves delicious pizzas and pasta dishes, made with fresh ingredients and cooked in a wood-fired oven.
10. Le Bistrot Gourmand - a cozy bistro that serves traditional French cuisine with a modern twist. Their beef tartare and sea bass are highly recommended.

When it comes to cafes, Nice is home to several historic and charming spots. Be sure to visit Café de Flore, a historic café that has been serving coffee and pastries since 1880. Café des Chineurs is a cozy cafe that serves organic and fair-trade coffee and homemade pastries. And for a stunning view of the sea, visit Le Plongeoir, a stylish rooftop bar and restaurant that offers panoramic views of the Mediterranean.

Overall, Nice's culinary scene is a must-try when visiting the city. So be sure to explore as many restaurants and cafes as possible during your stay!

Bars and Nightlife

Nice has a vibrant nightlife scene, with a mix of bars, clubs, and live music venues that cater to all tastes and ages. Whether you're looking for a relaxing drink with friends or a night out on the town, Nice has plenty to offer.

Here are some of the best bars and nightlife spots in Nice:

1. Le Bar du Coin - a cozy bar that serves a wide selection of craft beers and cocktails, as well as light bites and snacks.
2. Le High Club - a popular nightclub that hosts local and international DJs, with a mix of electronic, hip hop, and pop music.

3. La Bodeguita - a lively Latin bar that serves cocktails and tapas, and hosts salsa dancing nights on weekends.
4. Shapko Bar - a jazz bar that features live music every night, with a mix of local and international musicians.
5. L'Effervescence - a stylish champagne bar that serves a wide selection of bubbly, as well as cocktails and snacks.
6. Le Comptoir Central Électrique - a hip bar that serves craft cocktails and beers, with a mix of indoor and outdoor seating.
7. Wayne's Bar - a popular sports bar that features multiple screens showing live sports events, with a wide selection of beers and pub food.
8. Ma Nolan's - an Irish pub that serves a wide selection of beers and pub food, with live music and sports events on weekends.
9. Blue Beach - a beachfront club that features a pool, lounge chairs, and a bar, with a mix of electronic and pop music.
10. Le Master Home - a gay bar that hosts regular themed parties and events, with a mix of electronic and pop music.

When it comes to nightlife, the city also hosts several festivals and events throughout the year, such as the Nice Jazz Festival, the Nice Carnival, and the Fête de la Musique.

Overall, Nice's nightlife scene is a must-experience when visiting the city. So be sure to explore as many bars and clubs as possible during your stay!

Wine Tasting and Vineyards in and around Nice

Nice and the surrounding region offer a plethora of opportunities for wine enthusiasts to indulge in *wine tasting* and explore the picturesque *vineyards* of the French Riviera. The region is known for its diverse range of wines, including crisp whites, fruity rosés, and full-bodied reds, produced from various grape varieties such as Rolle, Tibouren, and Mourvèdre.

Here are some popular vineyards and wine tasting experiences in and around Nice that you should consider adding to your itinerary:

1. Bellet Vineyards

Located in the hills just a short drive from Nice, the *Bellet Vineyards* are known for producing high-quality wines with unique flavors influenced by the region's microclimate and diverse terroir. The area is home to several wineries that offer guided tours and tastings. Some of the notable wineries in Bellet include:

- *Domaine de Toasc*: A family-run winery offering guided tours and tastings by appointment. Visit their website for more information: www.domainedetoasc.com.
- *Château de Crémat*: This historic winery features a stunning castle and offers guided tours, tastings, and wine workshops. Visit their website to book a tour: www.chateau-de-cremat.com.

2. Domaine Saint-Jean

Domaine Saint-Jean is a picturesque vineyard located about an hour's drive from Nice, near the medieval village of Saint-Jeannet. The vineyard offers guided tours and tastings, where you can sample their organic wines while enjoying the breathtaking views of the surrounding countryside. Advance booking is recommended. For more information, visit their website: www.domainesaintjean.com.

3. Wine Tasting Tours

For those who prefer a guided experience, there are several companies offering *wine tasting tours* that take you to some of the best vineyards and wineries in the region. These tours typically

Avenue Jean Médecin

Avenue Jean Médecin is one of the most famous shopping streets in Nice. The street runs from the Nice train station to the Place Masséna, and is home to a wide range of shops, cafes, and restaurants.

The street is known for its mix of high-end fashion boutiques, department stores, and local shops, making it a popular destination for both locals and tourists. Visitors can find everything from designer fashion and jewelry to local crafts and souvenirs.

Some of the most popular shops on Avenue Jean Médecin include Galeries Lafayette, a large department store that features a wide range of fashion brands and products; H&M, a popular fashion retailer; and Fnac, a store that offers a wide range of electronics, books, and music.

In addition to its shops, Avenue Jean Médecin is also home to several cafes and restaurants, making it a great destination for a leisurely afternoon or evening stroll. Visitors can enjoy a coffee or a meal while taking in the sights and sounds of the street.

One of the street's most iconic features is the Galeries Lafayette dome, a beautiful glass dome that covers the entrance to the department store. The dome is a popular spot for photos and has become a symbol of the street.

Old Town (Vieux Nice)

Old Town, or Vieux Nice, is one of the most charming areas of the city, with its narrow streets, colorful buildings, and lively atmosphere. The area is also home to a wide range of shops and markets, making it a popular destination for shoppers.

Visitors can find everything from local crafts and souvenirs to fresh produce and seafood at the markets. Some of the most popular markets in Old Town include the Cours Saleya Market and the Marché aux Fleurs, which offer a wide range of fresh produce, flowers, and other local specialties.

In addition to the markets, Old Town is also home to several shops that sell local crafts, such as pottery, textiles, and jewelry. Visitors can find **unique and handmade souvenirs** to take back home with them.

One of the most popular shops in Old Town is Auer, a family-owned confectionery that has been in business since 1820. The shop is known for its delicious candied fruits and chocolates, and is a **must-visit destination for anyone with a sweet tooth**.

Old Town is also home to several fashion boutiques and shops, where visitors can find **unique and trendy fashion items**. Some of the most popular shops in the area include Coton Doux, which offers a range of colorful and stylish clothing items, and Yarinka, a boutique that features **unique and handmade clothing and accessories**.

Overall, shopping in Old Town is a **must-do when visiting Nice**. Whether you're looking for local crafts, fresh produce, or unique fashion items, Old Town has something to offer for every taste and budget.

Markets and Souvenirs

Nice is home to several markets that offer a wide range of local products and souvenirs. Visitors can find everything from fresh produce and seafood to local crafts and souvenirs.

One of the most popular markets in the city is the Cours Saleya Market, located in the heart of the Old Town. The market offers a wide range of fresh produce, flowers, and local specialties, such as olive oil, honey, and spices. Visitors can also find handmade crafts and souvenirs, such as pottery, textiles, and jewelry. The market is open every day except Monday, and is a **must-visit destination for anyone looking to experience the local culture**.

Another popular market in the city is the Marché aux Fleurs, located in the same area as the Cours Saleya Market. As the name suggests, the market specializes in flowers, with a wide range of seasonal blooms on offer. Visitors can also find other local products, such as herbs, soaps, and spices. The market is open every day except Monday, and is a **great place to buy a bouquet of flowers or a unique souvenir**.

For those looking for souvenirs, Nice is home to several shops that offer unique and handmade products. The Old Town is a great place to start, with its mix of local crafts and souvenirs. Visitors can find everything from pottery and textiles to jewelry and postcards. Some of the most popular souvenir shops in the area include Souvenir de la Provence, which offers a wide range of local products, and La Maison de la Lavande, which specializes in lavender products.

Art Galleries and Local Crafts in Nice

Nice has a thriving arts scene, with numerous galleries and local craft shops showcasing the diverse and vibrant talent of the region. From contemporary art to traditional crafts, the city offers a wide range of options for art enthusiasts and those looking to purchase unique, handmade souvenirs. Here are some notable art galleries and local craft shops in Nice to explore:

1. Galerie de la Marine

Located near the Old Port, the *Galerie de la Marine* is a contemporary art gallery managed by the city of Nice. The gallery hosts rotating exhibitions featuring the works of both established and emerging artists from the region and beyond. Entry is free, and the gallery is open from Tuesday to Sunday.

2. Musée d'Art Naïf Anatole Jakovsky

Dedicated to naïve art, the *Musée d'Art Naïf Anatole Jakovsky* is housed in the beautiful Château Sainte-Hélène. The museum showcases a diverse collection of paintings, sculptures, and other artworks by self-taught artists from around the world. Visit their website for more information: www.musee-art-naif-nice.org.

3. Galerie Eva Vautier

Galerie Eva Vautier is a contemporary art gallery located in the heart of Nice, featuring a wide range of exhibitions and installations by local and international artists. The gallery is known for its innovative approach to showcasing art and nurturing emerging talent. For more information, visit their website: www.galerieevavautier.com.

4. Poterie de la Madeleine

Poterie de la Madeleine is a local pottery studio and shop offering handmade ceramics, including tableware, decorative items, and unique gifts. Visitors can watch the artisans at work and purchase one-of-a-kind pieces to take home. Visit their website for more information: www.poterie-madeleine.com.

5. Les Ateliers du Parc Phoenix

Located within Phoenix Park, *Les Ateliers du Parc Phoenix* is a collective of local artists and artisans who create and sell a wide range of handmade crafts, including textiles, ceramics, glassware, and jewelry. The workshops offer visitors a chance to see the artists at work and purchase unique, locally made products.

6. Cours Saleya Market

The famous *Cours Saleya Market* in Nice's Old Town is not only known for its flowers and fresh produce but also for its vibrant arts and crafts section. Local artists and artisans sell their creations here, including paintings, sculptures, jewelry, and textiles, making it a perfect spot to find unique, handmade souvenirs.

Tips for Art and Craft Lovers in Nice

- Check the websites or social media pages of galleries and shops for information on current exhibitions, opening hours, and special events.
- When visiting galleries, remember to be respectful and follow any guidelines provided by the staff.
- When purchasing art or crafts, be prepared to pay in cash, as some smaller shops or market stalls may not accept credit cards.

Exploring Nice's art galleries and local craft shops is an excellent way to immerse yourself in the city's vibrant culture, support local artists, and bring home unique souvenirs that reflect the spirit of the French Riviera.

IV. Where to Stay in Nice

Nice has a wide range of accommodation options, from luxury hotels to budget hostels. When choosing where to stay, it's important to consider the location and what you want to see and do during your visit.

Here are some of the best areas to stay in Nice, along with their pros and cons, recommended hotels, and what to see in each area:

Old Town (Vieux Nice)

- Pros: charming atmosphere, close to markets and restaurants; Cons: noisy at night, limited parking options. Recommended hotels: Hôtel Rossetti, Hotel Suisse, Hotel Le Grimaldi. What to see: Cours Saleya Market, Place Masséna, Nice Cathedral.

Promenade des Anglais

- Pros: stunning views of the sea, easy access to beaches and restaurants; Cons: can be crowded during peak season, expensive accommodation. Recommended hotels: Hotel Negresco, Hyatt Regency Nice Palais de la Méditerranée, Le Méridien Nice. What to see: Castle Hill, Nice Opera, Blue Beach.

Carré d'Or

- Pros: central location, close to shopping and dining options; Cons: busy and noisy, limited parking options. Recommended hotels: Hotel Ellington, Hotel Windsor, Hotel West End. What to see: Avenue Jean Médecin, Place Masséna, Musée Masséna.

Port Area

- Pros: charming and authentic atmosphere, close to seafood restaurants and markets; Cons: limited accommodation options, can be noisy at night. Recommended hotels: Hôtel La Pérouse, Hotel Le Petit Palais, Villa Victoria. What to see: Port of Nice, Place Garibaldi, Mont Boron.

Cimiez

- Pros: peaceful and residential area, close to museums and gardens; Cons: limited dining and shopping options, far from the city center. Recommended hotels: Hotel Cimiez, Villa Saint Exupéry Beach Hostel, Hotel Apogia Nice. What to see: Musée Matisse, Musée Marc Chagall, Jardin des Arènes de Cimiez.

Overall, each area has its own unique features and advantages, so it's important to choose the one that best fits your needs and preferences. Consider what you want to see and do during your visit, and choose the area that will offer you the most convenient and enjoyable experience.

Our Recommended Hotel

Our recommendation is Hotel de la Fontaine; The Hotel De La Fontaine is a charming boutique hotel located in the heart of the Old Town, just a few steps away from the Cours Saleya Market and the Promenade des Anglais. The hotel is housed in a beautiful historic building and offers comfortable and cozy rooms, each with its own unique character.

The hotel's rooms are equipped with all the necessary amenities, including air conditioning, free Wi-Fi, and a flat-screen TV. The hotel also offers a continental breakfast, which can be enjoyed in the hotel's courtyard or in the comfort of your room.

One of the main advantages of the Hotel De La Fontaine is its location in the heart of the Old Town. Guests can easily explore the charming streets and markets of the area, and enjoy the vibrant nightlife and dining options. The hotel is also just a short walk away from the beach and the Promenade des Anglais, making it a great choice for those looking to relax by the sea.

The hotel's main disadvantage is its lack of an elevator, which may be a challenge for those with mobility issues or heavy luggage. The hotel is also located on a busy street, which can be noisy at times.

The average prices for a night at the Hotel De La Fontaine range from €80 to €150, depending on the season and room type.

Overall, the Hotel De La Fontaine is a great choice for those looking for a charming and cozy accommodation option in the heart of the Old Town. Its central location, comfortable rooms, and reasonable prices make it a popular choice among travelers visiting Nice.

Hotel De La Fontaine Located at 49 Rue de France, 06000 Nice, the Hotel De La Fontaine can be reached at +33 (0)4 93 88 30 38 or via email at contact@hotel-fontaine.com. To check prices, read reviews, and make online bookings, please visit their website: Click here

Luxury Hotels

1. **Hotel Negresco**: This iconic 5-star hotel is located on the famous Promenade des Anglais, offering luxurious accommodations with stunning sea views. The hotel features elegantly decorated rooms, fine dining options, and a private beach. Visit their website for more information: www.hotel-negresco-nice.com.

2. **Hyatt Regency Nice Palais de la Méditerranée**: Situated along the Promenade des Anglais, this 5-star hotel boasts an art deco façade, a private beach, and a rooftop terrace with a heated pool. The hotel offers spacious, modern rooms and an on-site restaurant. Visit their website for more information: www.hyatt.com.

Mid-range Hotels

3. **Hotel La Pérouse**: Located near the Old Town and Castle Hill, this 4-star hotel offers comfortable rooms with balconies and sea views. Amenities include an outdoor pool, a rooftop terrace, and an on-site restaurant. Visit their website for more information: www.hotel-la-perouse.com.

4. **Best Western Plus Hôtel Masséna Nice**: This centrally located 4-star hotel features stylish rooms, a daily breakfast buffet, and a lounge bar. Major attractions such as Place Masséna and the Old Town are within walking distance. Visit their website for more information: www.bestwestern-massena-nice.com.

Budget Hotels

5. **Hôtel Monsigny**: This budget-friendly 3-star hotel is located in the Malaussena district, near the main shopping street, Avenue Jean Médecin. The hotel offers clean, modern rooms and a rooftop terrace with city views. Visit their website for more information: www.hotelmonsigny.com.

6. **Ibis Styles Nice Centre Gare**: Conveniently located near the Nice Ville train station, this 3-star hotel offers colorful, contemporary rooms with free Wi-Fi and breakfast included. The hotel is within walking distance to many attractions and restaurants. Visit their website for more information: www.accorhotels.com.

Vacation Rentals and Apartments

7. **Nice Pebbles**: This vacation rental company offers a range of stylish, well-equipped apartments in prime locations throughout Nice. Options include beachfront properties, apartments in the Old Town, and accommodations near the train station. Visit their website for more information: www.nicepebbles.com.

8. **Stay YNA Nice**: Specializing in boutique apartments, Stay YNA Nice offers a selection of unique, high-quality rentals in various locations across the city. Visit their website for more information: www.stayyna.com.

Campsites and Caravan Parks

9. **Camping Les Gorges du Loup**: Located about 20 km from Nice, this family-friendly campsite offers spacious pitches for tents and caravans, as well as mobile homes for rent. Amenities include a swimming pool, playground, and snack bar. Visit their

website for more information: www.camping-gorgesduloup.com.

10. **Camping La Vieille Ferme**: Situated in Villeneuve-Loubet, about 15 km from Nice, this campsite offers pitches for tents, caravans, and motorhomes, as well as mobile homes and bungalows for rent. Facilities include a swimming pool, children's play area, and an on-site restaurant. Visit their website for more information: www.camping-vieille-ferme.com.

V. Our 3-Day Travel Itinerary to Nice

If you're planning a trip to Nice and have limited time, a 3-day itinerary is a great way to see the city's top attractions and get a taste of its unique culture and charm. In just three days, you can explore the charming Old Town, stroll along the iconic Promenade des Anglais, indulge in some delicious Niçoise cuisine, and visit some of the city's top museums and galleries. Whether you're traveling solo, with friends or family, or on a romantic getaway, this 3-day itinerary will help you make the most of your time in Nice. So, get ready to experience the best of the French Riviera!

Day 1 in Nice

9:00am - Arrival at Nice Côte d'Azur International Airport.

This is a small and efficient airport, with just two runways. It is close to 4kms outside of Nice. Bear in mind that it does not have any shops selling SIM cards for the French mobile system. Moreover, many visitors had incidents of taxi overcharges; be careful when you grab a cab. You can get the train to the city center, which costs only 2 Euros but you will have to walk for 15 minutes. On the cons of this airport, the toilets are not clean, the personnel are quite slow (even rude sometimes) and do not speak English, and you may have to experience unnecessary queues. Getting through the passport control may take up to 45 minutes. If you are a smoker, bear in mind that there is no internal place to smoke. At the moment, the second terminal of the airport, Terminal 2, is under reconstruction, while the Terminal 1 has already been rebuilt. The restaurants of the airport are rather average, so we do not recommend that you eat here.

The website of the airport is http://www.nice.aeroport.fr/

9:30am

Once you've retrieved your luggage, head outside to catch a cab for a convenient door-to-door service. Taxi ranks can be found at both terminals of the airport. Alternatively, you can take bus number 98, which runs every 20 minutes and goes to the city center.

The taxi rates from Nice Airport to the city center range from 23-31 € during daytime hours (7:00 am - 6:00 pm) and from 28-33 € during nighttime hours (6:00 pm - 7:00 am), not including luggage supplements. Please note that these rates are approximate and may vary depending on traffic conditions. The final fare will be calculated based on the taximeter.

While pre-booking a taxi is an option (call +33 (0) 899 70 08 78), it is not necessary as there are plenty of taxis available at the airport for tourists.

More Information

10:30am - Arrival at Hotel De La Fontaine

Once you've freshened up and unpacked, it's time to start exploring the city! Consider purchasing the Cote D'Azure Card, which grants access to 180 activities, including museums, guided tours, and even a one-day trip to Saint Tropez from Nice. The card costs 45 euros and can be purchased here. However, whether or not to purchase the card ultimately depends on your individual plans and preferences. For example, if you're planning on taking the trip to Saint Tropez, which is worth 48 euros, then the card may be a worthwhile investment. Ultimately, we recommend considering the activities included and deciding whether they align with your itinerary before purchasing the card.

You can get it here.

12:00pm - La Promenade des Anglais

Stroll along the renowned Promenade des Anglais, a landmark street that stretches along the Mediterranean Sea and features palm trees, cycling and skating lanes, and exciting attractions. While there, be sure to visit nearby Parc Phoenix, which boasts a stunning botanical garden with over 2,500 plant species and a tropical greenhouse.

This 7km-long street has a fascinating history. In the 18th century, English aristocrats vacationed in Nice during the summer. However, a few harsh winters in the UK led to a surge of beggars in Nice, which had a more temperate climate. To provide these beggars with work, the aristocrats commissioned the construction of a long street by the sea, where they could enjoy the views.

Initially known as "The English Way," the street was renamed "La Promenade des Anglais" after Nice was annexed by France in 1860. Locals affectionately refer to it as "La Prom."

Sadly, the Promenade des Anglais was also the site of a tragic terrorist attack on July 14, 2016. A terrorist drove a large truck along the street, killing 86 people.

13:00pm - Lunch at Olive et Artichaut

This restaurant in the heart of Old Nice draws inspiration from the local market for its menu. Watch the chef prepare fresh, locally sourced ingredients right in front of you at the open kitchen corner. Main courses range from 16 to 20 euros, so a meal for two could cost around 80 euros, unless you opt for a main course and a glass of wine, which could bring the cost down to 50 euros for two. We highly recommend trying the pork cotelettes. The service at this restaurant is also top-notch.

Check out Restaurant Olive et Artichaut, located at 6 Rue Sainte-Reparate, 06300. To make a reservation, give them a call at +33 4 89 14 97 51 or visit their website at www.oliveartichaut.com.

The restaurant is closed on Mondays and Tuesdays, but open for lunch from 12-2PM and for dinner from 7:30-10PM on all other days.

15:00pm - Visit the Musée Matisse

Spend your afternoon enjoying some beautiful art from the most famous artist of Nice, Henri Matisse. The Museum of Matisse is located in an olive grove and features the work of the famous French artist Henri Matisse, including oil paintings, drawings, sculptures, tapestries and Matisse's famous paper cut-outs. Be careful; the ticket office closes at 17:30 and will not let you get in if you arrive later, even though the museum operates until 18:00 PM. Our opinion on this museum is that it is an average museum and does do a great job in displaying the work of Matisse; for example, the lighting on the paintings of Matisse is not on par with the quality and the fame of the painter. Moreover, it does not offer a huge collection of Matisse paintings. We recommend it because we believe it is an interesting place to spend 60 to 90 minutes. You can also enjoy a coffee in the park after your visit to the museum. Moreover, the entry ticket is 10 euros, which is a fair price to pay to enjoy Matisse's work.

Two famous artworks of Matisse that you can enjoy here are *"Fleurs et Fruits"* and *"Les Abeilles."*

Fleurs et fruits, 1952/1953

Musee Matisse, Address: 164 Avenue des Arènes de Cimiez, 06000| Phone: +33 4 93 81 08 08| www.musee-matisse-nice.org

Opening Hours: Tuesday: Closed| All other days: Open from 10 AM until 6 PM, Entry Ticket: 10 euros. Free for students.

17:00pm - Tran Côte d'Azur boat cruise

Enjoy a guided boat cruise along the Baie des Anges and the Bay of Villefranche-sur-Mer to discover great landscapes and magnificent villas.

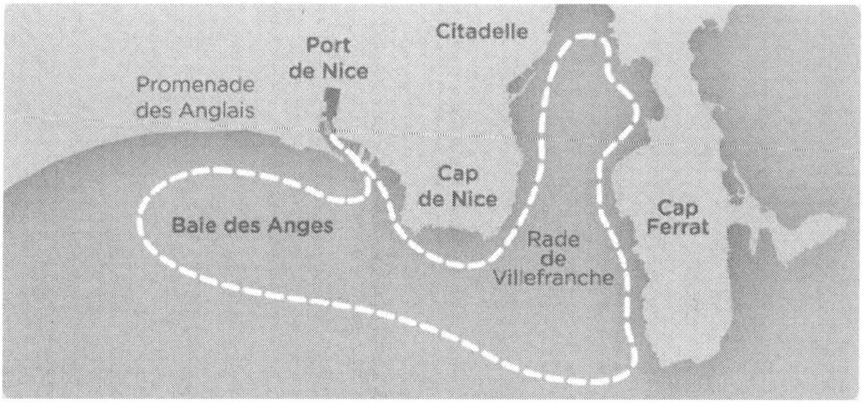

The cost per adult is 18 euros, and the duration is one hour. The boat leaves two times per day from the Port of Nice, and at the time of our research, there was one at 17:00 pm. Please make sure to check again, as this is subject to change. This company also offers day trips (8 hours each) to other popular places close to Nice, e.g. Iles Des Lerins, Ile Saint Marguerite, Monaco, Saint Tropez and Cannes.

Tran Cote D'Azure Cruise, Phone: +33 6 19 20 49 73, croisieres@trans-cote-azur.com, http://www.trans-cote-azur.com

19:30pm - Dinner at Vinivore

For a classic French dinner, head to Vinivore, a bistro-style restaurant for wine amateurs. Choose among the 200 different wines to accompany your dish and enjoy the friendly and casual service.

Restaurant Vinivore| Address: 10 Rue Lascaris, 06300 | Phone: +33 4 93 14 68 09| https://www.facebook.com/Vinivore-Le-Bistrot-347567565287880/

Day 1 – Online Map

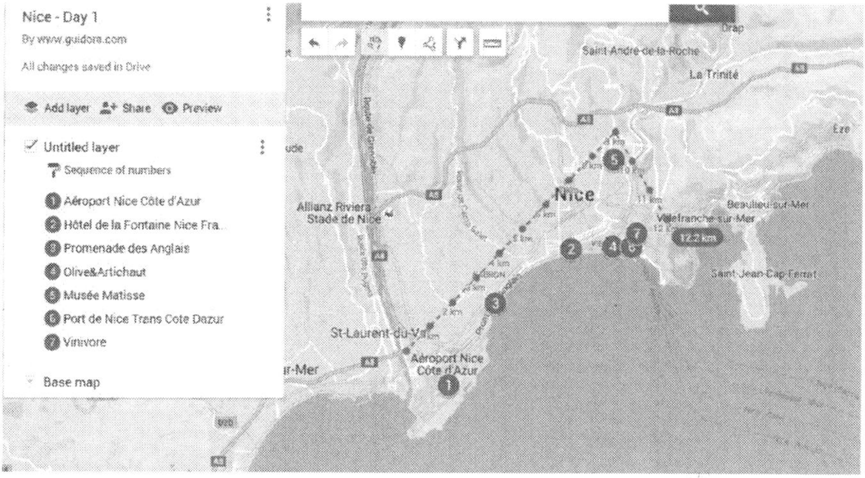

Welcome to our Google Map for a 3-day itinerary in Nice! This map is designed to help you make the most of your first day in the city. From the iconic Promenade des Anglais to the charming streets of the Old Town, this itinerary will take you to some of the most popular and must-see attractions in Nice. We've also included recommendations for local restaurants and cafes, as well as tips on transportation and other helpful information. So, let's get started and explore the best of Nice!

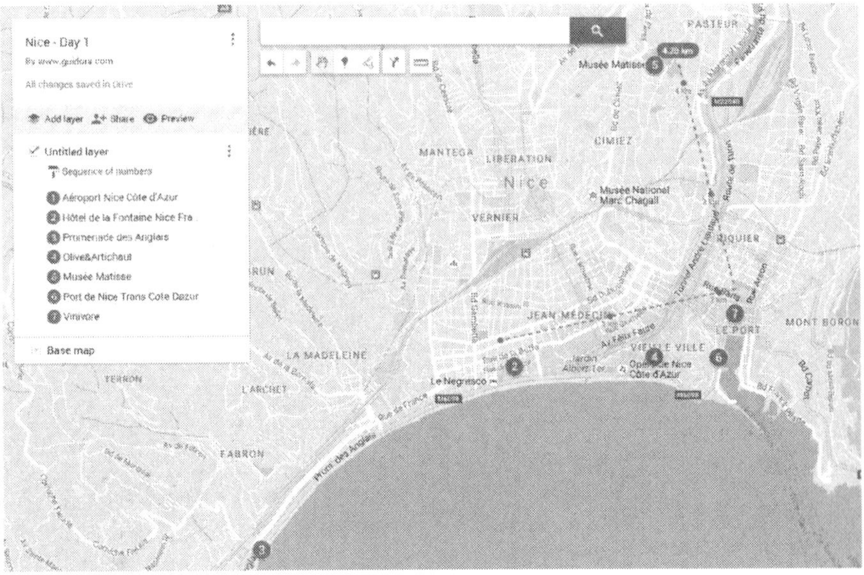

[Click here to Access the Online Google Map](#)

Day 2 in Nice

10:00 am - Tour of Nice with a Segway, Bike or On Foot.

After a buffet breakfast in your hotel, discover Nice by Segway. Explore its many pedestrian areas, parks, squares, and gardens. Learn about the city's 2500 years of history and culture with a licensed tour guide.

The Segway 2-hour Tour costs 50 euros per person, and you can book it here.

If two hours on Segway is too much for you, you can also get the one-hour tour, which costs 30 euros per person, here.

If you do not like Segways, you can just get a **Walking Tour of Nice**. It costs 14 euros per person; it has a duration of 100 minutes, and you can book it here.

Finally, if you are a bike lover, you can get a **Bike Tour of Nice**. It costs 29 euros per person; the tour duration is 3 hours, and you can book it here.

12:00pm - Lunch at Café de Turin

Nice is famous for its seafood. This brasserie-style restaurant featuring Nice's best oysters and seafood platters is located near the port. You should try the seafood liver, the Moules-Frites. It has some platters with a variety of seafood, which cost 33 euros and even though they are supposed to be for one person, you could share. Here, you can also get a free wi-fi connection.

Café De Turin

Address: 5 Place Garibaldi, 06300| Telephone: +33 4 93 62 29 52| www.cafedeturin.fr | Opening Times:Monday to Sunday: from 8 AM to 11 PM| Website: http://www.nice.fr/fr/culture/musees-et-galeries/musee-d-archeologie-site-de-cimiez-et-de-terra-amata-presentation

14:00pm - Head to the Musée Archéologique

Learn about the history of Roman city Cemenelum through a collection of objects dating from the 1st to the 5th century. Discover the fascinating ruins including the amphitheater, the baths, and the sewage trenches. This museum is small and fairly interesting, due to the ruins that you will see. You can get a 48 hours pass to all museums of Nice with 10 euros per person; more information at http://www.nice.fr/fr/culture/musees-et-galeries/preparer-ma-visite

Musee Archeologique| Address: 160 Avenue des Arènes de Cimiez, 06000 | Telephone: +33 4 93 81 59 57| Opening Hours: Daily from 10 AM to 6 PM

16:30pm - Stroll down at the Parc de la Colline du Château

Visit the most famous public garden of Nice. Set on the remains of an ancient citadel, this park offers a magnificent view of the old town and the port. This is a great spot for taking pictures. The Parc de la Colline du Chateau offers the best view of the French Riviera, and here you can have a picnic, eat some ice cream at a little café that is located inside the park and let your kids enjoy its lovely playground. This park also has a beautiful waterfall.

Website: https://www.nice.fr/fr/parcs-et-jardins/le-parc-de-la-colline-du-chateau

19:00pm - Have an aperitif and dinner at Chez Pippo

1 Socca coming out from the oven

This charming restaurant serves some of Nice's best socca, a tasty chickpea flour pancake. Enjoy the charm and authenticity of this notorious bistro located near the port. The dishes and the prices here are small. It is more like a "Tapas" place, with many different small dishes to try. Try the socca, the pisaladiere and the rose.

It is a kind of busy place, so don't be in a hurry as the service will be somewhat slow. You may also need to wait in a line to get a table. For a double socca, salad and drink you will pay around 10 to 12 euros.

Chez Pipo| Address: 13 Rue Bavastro, 06000| Telephone: +33 4 93 55 88 82| Opening Times: Monday: Closed, Tuesday to Saturday: Open from 11:30 AM to 2:30 PM and from 5:30 PM to 10 PM, Sunday: Open from 5:30 PM to 10 PM| Website: http://www.chezpipo.fr/

21:30pm - Enjoy a night in the town at the Bar de la Réserve

The champagne bar on the top floor of the La Réserve restaurant bar is perfect for anyone who wants to dance and enjoy tapas while taking in the sites of the nearby port, including a panoramic view of the Baie des Anges.

Please note that this restaurant is quite pricey, so be sure to budget accordingly. A typical meal here could cost around 70-80 euros per person. If you're looking for a more budget-friendly option, we recommend checking out the champagne bar on the rooftop instead.

Bar De La Reserve

Address: 60 boulevard Franck Pilatte, 06300, Telephone: +33 4 97 08 14 80, Reservations: https://www.lafourchette.com/restaurant/la-reserve-de-nice/8832?cc=18174-54f

Website: http://www.lareservedenice.fr/fr/

Opening Time: 18:30 to 00:00

Day 2 – Online Map

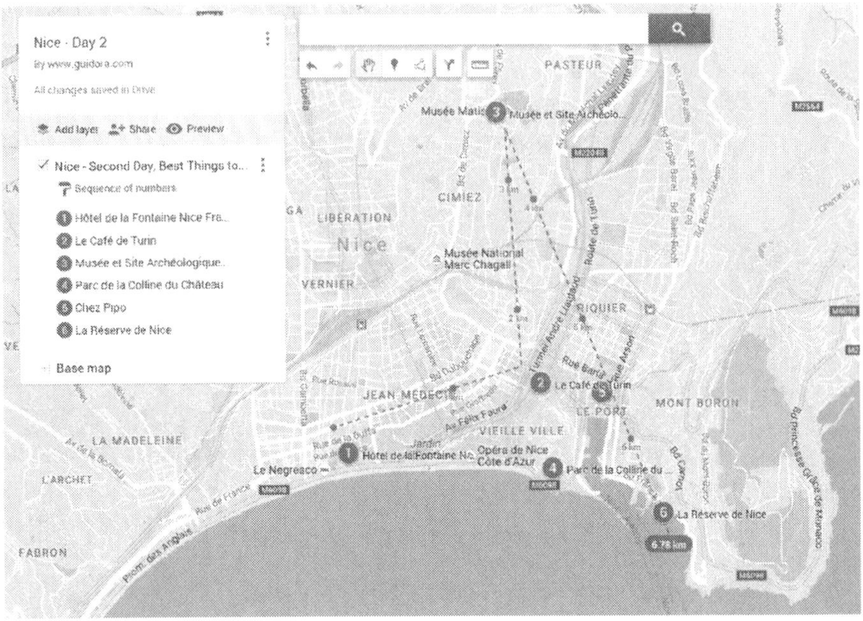

>> Click Here to Access The Online Google Map with All the Spots of the Second Day in Nice

Day 3 in Nice

9:00 am - People watch in Cours Saleya

This morning is all about exploring Vieux Nice, the ancient part of the city. Grab a quick bite at a boulangerie on your way down the colorful rue Droite taking in the Eglise de Jésus, and the Palais Lascars are on your way. You will notice that street signs are written both in French and in the local Nissart dialect. Be sure to check out the beautiful Cathédrale de Sainte Réparte, which was built in the 17th century. Once you are in Cours Saleya, the thriving pulse of Vieux Nice, sit down in a local café to take in the lively scene.

11:00 am - Shop for souvenirs and treats

Vieux Nice is the perfect spot to shop for trinkets and gifts for friends and family back home. You can find handmade jewelry at ***Les Delices de Candice*** (16 Rue de la Préfecture, 06300 Nice, France, +33 4 93 53 05 21) or art prints at the concept store ***La Briqueterie*** (4 - 6 Rue Jules Gilly, 06300 Nice). You will find tasty treats at the ***Patisserie Lac*** (18 Rue Barla, 06000 Nice).

13:00 pm - Lunch at Jan

At 1:00 pm, treat yourself to a delicious South African-inspired meal with a French twist at Jan restaurant. Located near the port, this intimate and romantic restaurant offers fresh, seasonal-based dishes instead of an à la carte menu. Be sure to save room for dessert from the famous Fenocchio parlor.

Jan restaurant has been awarded a Michelin star and is on the expensive side. For the menu without wine, expect to pay around 80 euros per person, while the full menu with wine could cost around 115 euros per person. However, if you come for lunch, the prices are more reasonable:

- Two courses: around 30 euros
- Two courses with wine: around 48 euros
- Three courses: around 42 euros
- Three courses with wine: around 62 euros

While we love food, we don't believe that a couple should spend 230 euros on dinner with wine. Instead, we recommend coming to Jan for lunch, where a meal for two can cost around 80-100 euros. For that amount, the experience is certainly worth it.

Restaurant Jan, is located at 12 Rue Lascaris, 06300. You can visit their website at http://www.restaurantjan.com/english to learn more about their menu, which offers a delicious South African-inspired cuisine with a French twist.

Please note that the restaurant is closed on Sundays and Mondays, but open from 6:30-10 PM on Tuesdays, Wednesdays, and Thursdays. On Fridays and Saturdays, the restaurant is open for lunch from 12-2 PM and for dinner from 6:30-10 PM. Be sure to book a table in advance to secure your spot at this highly sought-after restaurant.

15:00 pm - Head to the beach

Beach lovers may be disappointed when they discover that the beaches of Nice are not like those you will find in many seaside cities. Expect to find smooth pebbles instead of sandy beaches. Still, the beaches of Nice worth a visit to take in some sun and enjoy some watersports. The best public beach is the *Plage Publique de Beau Rivage*, which is a great spot for a picnic. Private beaches can cost anywhere from 10 to 18 euros per day, with the most luxurious being the Plage Beau Rivage.

20:00 pm - Enjoy your last dinner in Nice at Tapaloca and end with a night of music

After an afternoon spent lounging at the beach, head back to your hotel to clean up before going out for dinner on the town. A good dinner option is Tapaloca, a tapas bar known for its reasonable prices and quality fare.

After dinner, it is time to go dancing. Nightlife in Nice is alive and well. If you are a fan of live music, check out ***Acropolis***, (http://www.sean-acropolis.com/en/) a venue that offers shows featuring mainstream and underground artists.

If you prefer, you could dance the night away at the super trendy club ***Ghost*** *(3 Rue Barillerie, 06300 Nice; open daily from 11 PM to 4 AM, closed on Sunday, http://www.leghost-pub.com/),* a tiny spot that offers an eclectic mix of tunes. Whichever you choose, you are sure to end your last night in Nice with a bang.

Tapaloca Restaurant| https://www.facebook.com/tapaloca.nice | Address: 7 Rue du Pont Vieux, 06300 Nice| Opening Times: Everyday from 7 PM to 12:30 AM| Reviews and Booking: https://www.lafourchette.com/restaurant/tapaloca/39142

Day 3 – Online Map

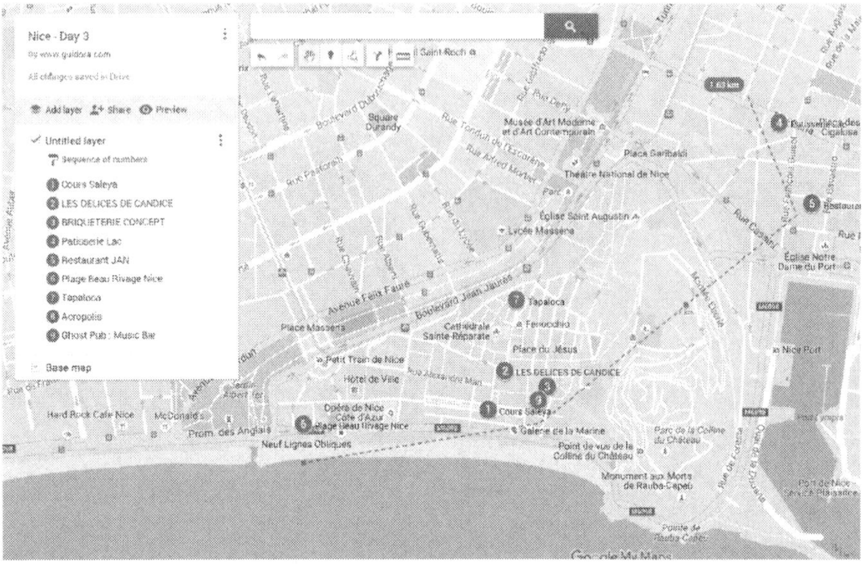

>> <u>Click Here to Access The Online Google Map for the Third Day in Nice</u>

A Second Option for a 3-Day Travel Itinerary to Nice

Here is a second option for a 3-day trip to Nice.

Day 1:

- 8:00 AM - Arrive at Nice Côte d'Azur Airport and head to the taxi stand to take a cab to your hotel.
- 9:00 AM - Check-in at your hotel and freshen up.
- 10:00 AM - Head to the Promenade des Anglais and take a stroll along the beachfront.
- 11:00 AM - Visit Castle Hill (Colline du Château) for stunning views of Nice.
- 12:00 PM - Lunch at Olive et Artichaut, a restaurant that offers fresh, locally sourced ingredients in the heart of Old Nice.
- 2:00 PM - Explore the charming streets of Old Town (Vieux Nice) and visit the Cours Saleya Flower Market.
- 4:00 PM - Visit the Musée Matisse and admire the works of this famous artist.
- 6:00 PM - Enjoy a glass of champagne at the rooftop bar of Hotel Le Negresco.
- 8:00 PM - Dinner at La Petite Maison, a restaurant that offers a delicious Mediterranean cuisine.
- 10:00 PM - Experience the nightlife of Nice at Les Caves du Roy.

Time	Activity	Website	Cost per Person
8:00 AM	Arrive at Airport	N/A	N/A
9:00 AM	Check-in at Hotel	N/A	N/A
10:00 AM	Promenade des Anglais	N/A	N/A
11:00 AM	Castle Hill	N/A	N/A
12:00 PM	Lunch at Olive et Artichaut	http://oliveartichaut.com/	30-62 Euros
2:00 PM	Old Town	N/A	N/A
4:00 PM	Musée Matisse	https://www.musee-matisse-nice.org/fr	10 Euros
6:00 PM	Hotel Le Negresco	https://www.hotel-negresco-nice.com/	N/A
8:00 PM	Dinner at La Petite Maison	https://www.lapetitemaison-nice.com/	70-100 Euros
10:00	Les Caves	https://www.lescavesduroy.com/nice/	Cover

Time	Activity	Website	Cost per Person
PM	du Roy		charge

Day 2:

- 9:00 AM - Have breakfast at your hotel.
- 10:00 AM - Visit the Musée Marc Chagall to see the works of this famous artist.
- 12:00 PM - Lunch at Jan restaurant, an intimate and romantic restaurant that offers a delicious South African-inspired cuisine with a French twist.
- 2:00 PM - Visit the Musée d'Art Moderne et d'Art Contemporain (MAMAC) to see contemporary art.
- 4:00 PM - Take a walk through Phoenix Park (Parc Phoenix) and enjoy the botanical garden with over 2,500 different plants.
- 6:00 PM - Head back to your hotel and relax for a bit.
- 8:00 PM - Dinner at Keisuke Matsushima, a restaurant that offers a fusion of Japanese and French cuisine.
- 10:00 PM - Enjoy the nightlife at Wayne's Bar.

Time	Activity	Website	Cost per Person
8:00 AM	Breakfast at hotel	N/A	N/A
9:00 AM	Explore Nice Port	N/A	N/A

Time	Activity	Website	Cost per Person
10:00 AM	Visit Chateau de Bellet Winery	https://www.chateau-bellet.com/	25 Euros
12:00 PM	Lunch at Les Pecheurs	https://www.les-pecheurs.com/	50-80 Euros
2:00 PM	Phoenix Park and Botanical Garden	https://www.parc-phoenix.org/	5 Euros
4:00 PM	Visit Musée Marc Chagall	https://www.musees-nationaux-alpesmaritimes.fr/chagall/	10 Euros
6:00 PM	Return to Hotel and freshen up	N/A	N/A
8:00 PM	Dinner at Keisuke Matsushima	https://www.keisukematsushima.com/	80-130 Euros
10:00 PM	Visit Le Ghost Club	https://www.leghostclub.fr/	Cover charge

Day 3:

- 9:00 AM - Have breakfast at your hotel.
- 10:00 AM - Visit Nice Cathedral (Cathédrale Sainte-Réparate) to see the beautiful Baroque architecture.
- 11:00 AM - Take a walk along Avenue Jean Médecin for some shopping.
- 1:00 PM - Lunch at Bistrot d'Antoine, a restaurant that offers traditional Niçoise cuisine.
- 3:00 PM - Visit Place Masséna, the city's main square, for some people-watching and photo opportunities.
- 4:00 PM - Walk to Rue De France for some more shopping.

- 6:00 PM - Head back to your hotel and freshen up for the evening.
- 8:00 PM - Dinner at Les Pêcheurs, a restaurant that offers fresh seafood with a beautiful seaside view.
- 10:00 PM - End your trip with a nightcap at L'Effervescence.

Time	Activity	Website	Cost per Person
8:00 AM	Breakfast at hotel	N/A	N/A
9:00 AM	Nice Flower Market (Cours Saleya)	N/A	N/A
10:00 AM	Visit Musée d'Art Moderne et d'Art Contemporain (MAMAC)	https://www.mamac-nice.org/	10 Euros
12:00 PM	Lunch at Boccaccio	https://www.boccaccio.fr/	25-50 Euros
2:00 PM	Walk around Rue de France	N/A	N/A
4:00 PM	Musée Marc Chagall	https://www.musees-nationaux-alpesmaritimes.fr/chagall/	10 Euros
6:00 PM	Return to Hotel and freshen up	N/A	N/A
8:00 PM	Dinner at Le Chantecler	https://www.royal-riviera.com/restaurant-le-chantecler/	150-200 Euros
10:00 PM	Nightlife at Le Glam	https://www.leglam.fr/	Cover charge

Alternative Activities and Attractions in Nice

For those seeking unique experiences beyond the typical tourist attractions, Nice offers a variety of alternative activities and attractions that cater to diverse interests. Here are some lesser-known, yet equally enjoyable, options to explore during your visit:

1. Villa Ephrussi de Rothschild

Located in Saint-Jean-Cap-Ferrat, about a 30-minute drive from Nice, the *Villa Ephrussi de Rothschild* is a stunning Belle Époque mansion surrounded by nine themed gardens. Built by Baroness Béatrice de Rothschild, the villa showcases an impressive collection of artwork, furniture, and porcelain. The gardens, featuring fountains, sculptures, and rare plants, offer breathtaking views of the Mediterranean Sea. For more information, visit their website: www.villa-ephrussi.com.

2. Cimiez Monastery and Gardens

Situated in the Cimiez neighborhood, the *Cimiez Monastery and Gardens* is a peaceful oasis away from the bustling city center. The 16th-century Franciscan monastery houses a small museum with religious artifacts and artwork, while the adjacent cemetery is the final resting place of renowned painters Henri Matisse and Raoul Dufy. The beautifully manicured gardens offer panoramic views of Nice and are an ideal spot for a leisurely stroll or a picnic.

3. Parcours de santé du Mont Boron

For outdoor enthusiasts, the *Parcours de santé du Mont Boron* is a scenic fitness trail located within the Mont Boron Forest Park. The 2.5 km (1.5 miles) trail features exercise stations and offers stunning views of Nice, Villefranche-sur-Mer, and the Mediterranean Sea.

This is a perfect option for travelers looking to stay active while enjoying the natural beauty of the region.

4. Le 22 Gallery

Le 22 Gallery is a contemporary art gallery located in Nice's Old Town, featuring a wide range of artworks from local and international artists. The gallery hosts rotating exhibitions and events, making it an excellent destination for art enthusiasts seeking to discover emerging talent. Visit their website for more information: www.le22galerie.com.

5. Nice Street Art Walking Tour

Discover Nice's vibrant street art scene with a self-guided or guided walking tour, showcasing the city's most impressive murals and graffiti art. Several tour operators and online resources offer maps and itineraries that will take you through various neighborhoods, providing insights into the artists and their work.

6. La Maison du Chocolat

Indulge your sweet tooth with a visit to *La Maison du Chocolat*, a local chocolate boutique offering a delectable selection of handmade chocolates and confections. The shop frequently hosts chocolate-making workshops and tastings, providing a unique opportunity to learn about the art of chocolate making and sample their delicious creations. Visit their website for more information: www.lamaisonduchocolat.fr.

7. Guided Bike Tours

Explore Nice and its surroundings by bike with a guided tour tailored to your interests and fitness level. Several tour operators, such as *Nice Cycle Tours* (www.nicecycletours.com) and *Bike Trip* (www.biketrip.fr), offer a range of options, from leisurely city tours to more challenging rides through the surrounding hills and coastal roads.

8. La Chaise Bleue de SAB

For a truly unique souvenir or gift, visit *La Chaise Bleue de SAB*, a boutique dedicated to the iconic blue chairs that line the Promenade des Anglais. The shop offers a range of products featuring the distinctive blue chair design, including tote bags, clothing, and home decor items. The boutique also showcases original artwork and limited edition prints by local artists. Visit their website for more information: www.lachaisebleue.fr.

9. Le Sentier du Littoral

For a scenic coastal hike, explore *Le Sentier du Littoral*, a walking trail that stretches along the Cap d'Antibes peninsula. The trail offers stunning views of the Mediterranean Sea, secluded beaches, and beautiful villas. Along the way, you'll pass landmarks such as the *Phare de la Garoupe* lighthouse and the *Villa Eilenroc*, a magnificent Belle Époque mansion.

10. Le Petit Train de Nice

Take a break from walking and enjoy a leisurely ride on *Le Petit Train de Nice*, a small tourist train that takes you on a guided tour through Nice's historic neighborhoods, including the Old Town, Castle Hill, and the Promenade des Anglais. The train provides audio commentary in multiple languages, offering a fun and informative way to explore the city. Visit their website for more information: www.lepetittraindenice.com.

By venturing off the beaten path and exploring these alternative activities and attractions, visitors can experience a different side of

Nice, immersing themselves in the city's rich culture, history, and natural beauty. These lesser-known options offer unique experiences that will make your trip to Nice truly memorable.

VI. Excursions from Nice

While there's no shortage of things to see and do in Nice, the French Riviera has so much more to offer beyond the city limits. In this section, we will explore some of the best day trips and excursions that you can take from Nice to discover the surrounding region. Whether you're interested in exploring medieval villages, lounging on sandy beaches, or indulging in world-class wine and food, there's something for everyone just a short journey away from Nice. So pack your bags, hop on a train or bus, and let's embark on an adventure to discover the hidden gems of the Côte d'Azur.

Cannes

Cannes is a charming coastal city that lies just a short train ride away from Nice. Known for its glitz and glamour, Cannes is perhaps most famous for its annual international film festival, which draws in celebrities from all around the world. However, there's more to Cannes than just the red carpet. This beautiful city is home to a charming old town, where visitors can explore narrow streets and picturesque alleyways lined with restaurants, bars, and shops. The city is also famous for its beautiful beaches, where you can spend a lazy afternoon soaking up the Mediterranean sun.

One of the best ways to experience Cannes is to take a stroll along the famous Promenade de la Croisette, which offers stunning views of the Mediterranean Sea and is lined with luxury hotels, cafes, and shops. You can also take a boat ride out to the Lérins Islands, located just off the coast of Cannes, where you can explore a stunning natural reserve with crystal-clear waters and unspoiled landscapes.

Cannes is a great excursion from Nice for a day trip, and you can easily reach it by train from Nice's central train station. The journey takes about 30-40 minutes and costs around €7 each way. Whether you're a film buff, beach lover, or just looking for a change of scenery, Cannes is a great destination to explore on your visit to the French Riviera.

Antibes

Antibes is a charming coastal town that lies just a short train ride away from Nice. With its beautiful beaches, historic old town, and world-famous Picasso museum, Antibes is a must-visit destination for anyone exploring the French Riviera.

One of the main attractions in Antibes is the historic old town, which is filled with narrow streets, charming squares, and beautiful old buildings. Visitors can explore the bustling market, where vendors sell fresh produce, seafood, and handmade crafts. The old town is also home to the impressive Château Grimaldi, which now houses the Musée Picasso, a museum dedicated to the work of the famous artist.

Antibes is also home to several beautiful beaches, including the Plage de la Gravette, a small sandy cove located just a short walk from the old town. Visitors can also explore the Fort Carré, a 16th-century fortress located on a hilltop overlooking the town and the Mediterranean Sea.

To reach Antibes from Nice, you can take a short train ride from Nice's central train station. The journey takes about 20-30 minutes and costs around €4 each way. Whether you're interested in history, art, or just relaxing on the beach, Antibes is a great destination to explore on your visit to the French Riviera.

Monaco

Monaco is a small, independent city-state located along the French Riviera, just a short train ride away from Nice. Known for its glamorous casinos, luxury yachts, and stunning architecture, Monaco is a must-visit destination for anyone exploring the French Riviera.

One of the main attractions in Monaco is the famous Monte Carlo Casino, which was made famous by James Bond movies and attracts visitors from all over the world. Visitors can also explore the Prince's Palace of Monaco, which is home to the ruling Grimaldi family and offers stunning views of the Mediterranean Sea.

Monaco is also home to several beautiful gardens, including the Jardin Exotique, a botanical garden filled with exotic plants and cacti from around the world. Visitors can also explore the Oceanographic Museum, a stunning aquarium that houses a diverse collection of marine life, including sharks, turtles, and rays.

To reach Monaco from Nice, you can take a short train ride from Nice's central train station. The journey takes about 20-30 minutes and costs around €4 each way. Whether you're interested in luxury, history, or stunning natural landscapes, Monaco is a great destination to explore on your visit to the French Riviera.

Saint-Tropez

Saint-Tropez is a picturesque town located along the French Riviera, just a short drive or ferry ride away from Nice. With its beautiful beaches, historic old town, and lively nightlife, Saint-Tropez is a must-visit destination for anyone exploring the French Riviera.

One of the main attractions in Saint-Tropez is the historic old town, which is filled with narrow streets, charming squares, and beautiful old buildings. Visitors can explore the bustling market, where vendors sell fresh produce, seafood, and handmade crafts. The old town is also home to several stunning churches, including the Chapelle Sainte-Anne, a beautiful 16th-century chapel.

Saint-Tropez is also known for its beautiful beaches, including the Plage de Pampelonne, a stunning stretch of white sand that attracts sun-seekers from all over the world. Visitors can also explore the Musée de l'Annonciade, a museum dedicated to the work of the Impressionist painters who were drawn to Saint-Tropez in the early 20th century.

To reach Saint-Tropez from Nice, you can take a ferry from the Port of Nice, which takes about 2 hours and costs around €40 each way. Alternatively, you can drive to Saint-Tropez, which takes about 1.5 hours and offers stunning views of the French Riviera coastline. Whether you're interested in history, art, or just relaxing on the beach, Saint-Tropez is a great destination to explore on your visit to the French Riviera

Eze Village

Eze Village is a charming medieval village located in the hills above the French Riviera, just a short drive or bus ride away from Nice. With its cobbled streets, ancient stone houses, and stunning views of the Mediterranean Sea, Eze Village is a must-visit destination for anyone exploring the French Riviera.

One of the main attractions in Eze Village is the Jardin Exotique d'Eze, a beautiful botanical garden filled with exotic plants and stunning views of the coastline. Visitors can also explore the village's ancient stone buildings, including the 14th-century Chapelle de la

Sainte Croix and the Château de la Chèvre d'Or, a luxury hotel housed in a medieval castle.

Eze Village is also known for its artisan shops and galleries, where visitors can browse handmade crafts, art, and jewelry. The village's narrow streets and winding alleys are perfect for strolling and soaking up the atmosphere.

To reach Eze Village from Nice, you can take a bus from the Nice bus station, which takes about 45 minutes and costs around €1.50 each way. Alternatively, you can drive to Eze Village, which takes about 20 minutes and offers stunning views of the French Riviera coastline. Whether you're interested in history, nature, or just soaking up the atmosphere of a charming medieval village, Eze Village is a great destination to explore on your visit to the French Riviera.

Grasse

Grasse is a charming town located in the hills above the French Riviera, just a short drive or train ride away from Nice. Known as the perfume capital of the world, Grasse is home to several perfume factories and museums, as well as beautiful parks and historic landmarks.

One of the main attractions in Grasse is the Fragonard Perfume Factory, where visitors can take a guided tour of the factory and learn about the process of making perfume. The factory also has a museum dedicated to the history of perfume-making, as well as a shop where visitors can purchase perfumes and other beauty products.

Grasse is also home to several beautiful parks and gardens, including the Parc Communal de la Corniche Fleurie, which offers stunning views of the coastline, and the Jardin des Plantes, a botanical garden filled with exotic plants and flowers.

To reach Grasse from Nice, you can take a train from the Nice train station, which takes about 30 minutes and costs around €6 each way. Alternatively, you can drive to Grasse, which takes about 45 minutes and offers stunning views of the French Riviera coastline. Whether you're interested in perfume, nature, or just exploring a charming town, Grasse is a great destination to visit on your trip to the French Riviera.

Menton

Menton, often referred to as the "Pearl of France," is a charming coastal town located approximately 35 km (22 miles) east of Nice, near the Italian border. Renowned for its mild climate, lush gardens, and vibrant lemon festival, Menton is an ideal day trip destination that offers visitors a glimpse of the authentic charm and beauty of the French Riviera. Here's how to make the most of your excursion to Menton:

Getting There

The most convenient way to reach Menton from Nice is by train. The journey takes around 30-45 minutes, with frequent services running throughout the day. Check the train schedules and prices on the SNCF website: www.oui.sncf. Alternatively, you can take a bus (line 100) from Nice's bus station, which takes about 1.5 hours.

Top Attractions

1. **Old Town (Vieux Menton)**: Stroll through Menton's picturesque Old Town, featuring narrow, winding streets, pastel-colored houses, and a lively atmosphere. Don't miss the *Basilique Saint-*

Michel-Archange, a beautiful baroque church with an impressive façade and bell tower.

2. **Jardin Serre de la Madone**: One of Menton's most famous gardens, the *Jardin Serre de la Madone* is a lush, terraced garden showcasing a wide variety of exotic plants and flowers. Designed by landscape architect Lawrence Johnston, the garden offers stunning views of the Mediterranean Sea. Visit their website for more information: www.serredelamadone.com.

3. **Musée Jean Cocteau Collection Séverin Wunderman**: This museum is dedicated to the works of French artist and poet Jean Cocteau, featuring a vast collection of paintings, drawings, sculptures, and photographs. The museum is housed in a modern building near the seafront, designed by architect Rudy Ricciotti. Visit their website for more information: www.museecocteaumenton.fr.

4. **The Lemon Festival (Fête du Citron)**: If you're visiting Menton between mid-February and early March, don't miss the annual Lemon Festival, a vibrant celebration of Menton's citrus-growing heritage. The festival features colorful parades, citrus-themed sculptures, and various cultural events. Visit their website for more information: www.fete-du-citron.com.

Food and Drink

Menton offers a variety of dining options, from traditional French bistros to Italian-inspired restaurants. Be sure to try local specialties such as *barbajuan* (stuffed pastries) and *socca* (a chickpea flour pancake). For a unique dining experience with panoramic sea views, consider visiting *Mirazur*, a three-Michelin-starred restaurant helmed by Chef Mauro Colagreco. Visit their website for more information: www.mirazur.fr.

Tips for Your Excursion to Menton

- Wear comfortable shoes, as the Old Town's streets can be steep and uneven.
- Bring sunscreen and a hat, especially during the summer months when the sun can be intense.
- Don't forget your camera, as Menton offers picturesque views and charming scenery at every turn.

An excursion to Menton provides a delightful contrast to the bustling atmosphere of Nice, offering visitors the opportunity to experience the charm and beauty of a traditional French Riviera town. With its picturesque Old Town, beautiful gardens, and rich cultural heritage, Menton is a must-visit destination for travelers seeking a more relaxed and authentic experience.

Saint-Paul de Vence

Saint-Paul de Vence, a picturesque medieval village perched on a hilltop, is located approximately 25 km (15.5 miles) northwest of Nice. Renowned for its well-preserved ramparts, narrow cobblestone streets, and thriving art scene, this charming village has long attracted artists, writers, and celebrities seeking inspiration and tranquility. A day trip to Saint-Paul de Vence provides a unique opportunity to experience the rich history, culture, and natural beauty of the French Riviera's hinterland.

Getting There

The easiest way to reach Saint-Paul de Vence from Nice is by car, which takes about 30 minutes via the A8 motorway. Alternatively, you can take bus line 400 from Nice's bus station, which takes around 1 hour. Note that there is no direct train connection to the village.

Top Attractions

1. **Ramparts and Medieval Village**: Wander through the village's narrow, winding streets, lined with well-preserved stone buildings and adorned with vibrant flowers. Explore the 16th-century ramparts, which offer stunning panoramic views of the surrounding countryside and the Mediterranean Sea.

2. **Fondation Maeght**: This modern art museum, designed by Spanish architect Josep Lluís Sert, houses an impressive collection of works by renowned artists such as Matisse, Chagall, and Giacometti. The museum also features a sculpture garden and hosts temporary exhibitions. Visit their website for more information: www.fondation-maeght.com.

3. **Colombe d'Or**: A visit to Saint-Paul de Vence is not complete without stopping by the legendary *Colombe d'Or* hotel and restaurant. Over the years, this establishment has attracted numerous artists and celebrities, many of whom contributed artwork in exchange for meals or lodging. The walls of the restaurant are adorned with original works by Picasso, Matisse, and other celebrated artists.

4. **Local Art Galleries**: As you stroll through the village, take the time to visit the numerous art galleries showcasing a diverse range of works by local and international artists. From traditional landscapes to contemporary sculptures, Saint-Paul de Vence offers a vibrant and eclectic art scene.

Food and Drink

There are several excellent dining options in Saint-Paul de Vence, ranging from casual cafés to fine dining establishments. Be sure to sample regional specialties such as *socca* (chickpea flour pancake) and *pissaladière* (onion and anchovy tart). For a memorable dining experience with breathtaking views, consider *La Vague d'Or*, a Michelin-starred restaurant located at the *Le Saint-Paul Hotel*. Visit their website for more information: www.lesaintpaul.com.

Tips for Your Excursion to Saint-Paul de Vence

- Wear comfortable walking shoes, as the village's cobblestone streets can be uneven and steep.
- Bring a light jacket, as the hilltop location can result in cooler temperatures and breezes, especially during the evenings.
- Don't forget your camera, as Saint-Paul de Vence offers picturesque views and charming scenery at every turn.

An excursion to Saint-Paul de Vence offers visitors a unique opportunity to explore a beautifully preserved medieval village with a rich artistic heritage. Whether you're an art enthusiast, history lover, or simply seeking a peaceful retreat from the bustling coastal cities, Saint-Paul de Vence is a must-visit destination on the French Riviera.

Villa Ephrussi de Rothschild

The Villa Ephrussi de Rothschild, located in the prestigious Saint-Jean-Cap-Ferrat peninsula, is a magnificent Belle Époque mansion surrounded by nine beautifully landscaped gardens. Built by Baroness Béatrice de Rothschild between 1905 and 1912, the villa offers visitors a glimpse into the opulent lifestyle of the early 20th century European elite. With its stunning architecture, lavish interiors, and breathtaking views of the Mediterranean Sea, a visit to the Villa Ephrussi de Rothschild makes for an unforgettable excursion from Nice.

Getting There

The Villa Ephrussi de Rothschild is approximately 10 km (6 miles) east of Nice and can be easily reached by car in about 30 minutes via the Basse Corniche (D6098). Alternatively, you can take bus line 81 from Nice's bus station to the "Passable/Rothschild" stop, which is a short walk from the villa. The journey takes around 45 minutes to 1 hour. There is no direct train connection to the villa.

Top Attractions

1. **Villa and Art Collection**: Explore the villa's lavish rooms, adorned with fine furniture, artwork, and porcelain from the Baroness's personal collection. Highlights include the grand salon, dining room, and the impressive music room, featuring a rare 18th-century Gobelins tapestry.

2. **Nine Themed Gardens**: Designed by landscape architect Achille Duchêne, the villa's gardens are organized into nine distinct themes: French, Spanish, Florentine, Stone, Japanese, Exotic, Rose, Provençal, and Sèvres. Each garden offers a unique atmosphere and features a variety of plants, sculptures, and fountains.

3. **Musical Fountains**: Don't miss the villa's enchanting musical fountains, which operate on a schedule during the high season. Set to classical music, the fountains provide a mesmerizing and romantic backdrop for your visit to the gardens.

4. **Tea Room and Gift Shop**: After exploring the villa and gardens, relax in the on-site tea room, which offers light refreshments,

snacks, and a selection of beverages. The gift shop is the perfect place to pick up a souvenir or gift inspired by the villa and its gardens.

Tips for Your Excursion to Villa Ephrussi de Rothschild

- Wear comfortable walking shoes, as you'll be spending a considerable amount of time exploring the villa's gardens.
- Bring sunscreen, a hat, and sunglasses, as the gardens offer limited shade during sunny days.
- Don't forget your camera, as the villa and gardens provide countless photo opportunities, from the opulent interiors to the stunning sea views.

Visiting Hours and Admission

The Villa Ephrussi de Rothschild is open daily, with varying hours depending on the season. For updated visiting hours and admission prices, visit their website: www.villa-ephrussi.com.

An excursion to the Villa Ephrussi de Rothschild offers visitors a unique opportunity to experience the luxurious lifestyle of the early 20th-century European elite while enjoying the beauty and tranquility of the villa's magnificent gardens. With its rich history, stunning architecture, and breathtaking views, a visit to this Belle Époque gem is a must for anyone exploring the French Riviera.

Gorges du Verdon

The Gorges du Verdon, also known as the Grand Canyon of Europe, is an awe-inspiring natural wonder situated in the heart of the Verdon Regional Natural Park. With its dramatic limestone cliffs, turquoise river, and verdant forests, the Gorges du Verdon is a must-visit destination for nature lovers and adventure enthusiasts looking for a memorable excursion from Nice.

Getting There

The Gorges du Verdon is located about 160 km (100 miles) northwest of Nice. The most convenient way to reach the area is by car, which takes approximately 2.5 to 3 hours, depending on the route. Public transportation options are limited and can be time-consuming, so renting a car is highly recommended.

Top Attractions

1. **Driving the Gorges du Verdon**: The scenic drive around the gorges offers breathtaking views and numerous photo opportunities. Two main routes are available: the northern route, known as Route des Crêtes, and the southern route, known as Corniche Sublime. Each route offers unique perspectives of the canyon, so consider driving both for the full experience.

2. **Hiking**: The Gorges du Verdon offers numerous hiking trails suitable for all levels of fitness and experience. Popular trails include the *Sentier Martel*, a challenging 15 km (9.3 miles) hike through the heart of the canyon, and the *Sentier de l'Imbut*, a shorter but equally spectacular trail that takes you to a hidden waterfall.

3. **Water-based Activities**: The Verdon River and the nearby Lac de Sainte-Croix provide opportunities for various water-based activities, such as kayaking, canoeing, paddleboarding, and white-water rafting. Equipment rental and guided tours are available from local outfitters.

4. **Rock Climbing**: The Gorges du Verdon is a world-famous rock climbing destination, with over 1,500 climbing routes catering to all skill levels. Local climbing schools and guides are available for those looking to explore the cliffs safely.

Tips for Your Excursion to Gorges du Verdon

- Wear comfortable walking shoes, as many of the best viewpoints and attractions require a short hike.
- Bring sunscreen, a hat, and sunglasses, as the sun can be intense, especially during the summer months.
- Pack a picnic lunch, as dining options within the park can be limited.
- Plan ahead and start early, as the drive from Nice is relatively long, and you'll want to have ample time to explore the area.

Visiting Hours and Admission

The Gorges du Verdon is open year-round, and there is no admission fee to enter the park. However, some attractions and activities within the park may have fees or require advanced reservations.

For a truly unforgettable experience, plan an excursion to the Gorges du Verdon, one of Europe's most spectacular natural wonders. Whether you're seeking breathtaking vistas, exhilarating hikes, or thrilling water sports, the Gorges du Verdon offers an abundance of opportunities to explore and connect with nature.

VII.Useful Phrases

When traveling to a foreign country, it is important to know some basic phrases in the local language. Not only does it show respect to the locals, but it can also make your travel experience smoother and more enjoyable. In this guide, we will cover some useful phrases that will help you navigate your way through Nice, France.

Greetings and Introductions

- Bonjour – Hello (used during the day)
- Bonsoir – Good evening (used in the evening)
- Comment ça va? – How are you?
- Je m'appelle... – My name is...
- Enchanté – Nice to meet you
- Au revoir – Goodbye

Asking for Help and Directions

- Je ne parle pas français – I don't speak French
- Pouvez-vous m'aider? – Can you help me?
- Où se trouve...? – Where is...?
- Comment aller à...? – How do I get to...?
- Excusez-moi – Excuse me
- Je suis perdu(e) – I am lost

Ordering Food and Drinks

- Je voudrais... – I would like...
- Qu'est-ce que vous recommandez? – What do you recommend?
- L'addition, s'il vous plaît – The bill, please
- Un verre de vin rouge/blanc – A glass of red/white wine
- Une carafe d'eau – A carafe of water

- Je suis végétarien(ne) – I am vegetarian
- Je suis allergique à... – I am allergic to...

Shopping

- Combien ça coûte? – How much is it?
- Pouvez-vous baisser le prix? – Can you lower the price?
- Je cherche... – I am looking for...
- Avez-vous ceci en taille...? – Do you have this in size...?
- Je vais réfléchir – I will think about it

Emergencies

- Aidez-moi! – Help me!
- Police! – Police!
- Feu! – Fire!
- Je suis malade – I am sick
- Où est l'hôpital le plus proche? – Where is the nearest hospital?

Other Useful Phrases

- Merci – Thank you
- De rien – You're welcome
- Excusez-moi – Excuse me
- Je suis désolé(e) – I am sorry
- Parlez-vous anglais? – Do you speak English?
- Je comprends – I understand
- Je ne comprends pas – I don't understand

Learning some basic French phrases will not only make your travel experience smoother and more enjoyable, but it can also help you connect with the locals and immerse yourself in the culture. Don't be afraid to practice your French with the locals – they will appreciate your effort and may even be willing to help you improve your language skills. With these useful phrases in your back pocket, you're ready to navigate your way through Nice, France with confidence.

IX. Travel Tips and Resources

Safety Tips

- Stay aware of your surroundings, especially in crowded tourist areas, as pickpocketing can occur.
- Avoid carrying large amounts of cash or wearing flashy jewelry.
- Keep your belongings secure and use hotel safes for valuable items.
- Stick to well-lit, populated areas when walking at night.
- Do not leave your drink unattended at bars or restaurants.
- Familiarize yourself with the local emergency numbers (112 for general emergencies, 15 for medical emergencies, 17 for police, and 18 for fire).

Public Holidays and Events

- New Year's Day (January 1)
- Easter Monday (date varies)
- Labor Day (May 1)
- Victory Day (May 8)
- Ascension Day (date varies)
- Whit Monday (date varies)
- Bastille Day (July 14)
- Assumption of Mary (August 15)

- All Saints' Day (November 1)
- Armistice Day (November 11)
- Christmas Day (December 25)
- Nice Carnival (February, dates vary)
- Nice Jazz Festival (July, dates vary)

Currency and Money Matters

- The currency in Nice is the Euro (€).
- ATMs are widely available, but inform your bank of your travel plans to avoid blocked transactions.
- Credit cards are widely accepted, but it's a good idea to carry some cash for smaller purchases.
- Tipping is not obligatory in France, but it's customary to leave a small tip (1-2€) for good service in restaurants and cafes.

Internet and Communication

- Most hotels, cafes, and restaurants offer free Wi-Fi, but connection speeds may vary.
- Consider purchasing a local SIM card or using an international data plan for reliable internet access during your trip.
- To call France from abroad, dial +33 followed by the local number (without the initial 0).

Healthcare and Medical Emergencies

- Ensure your travel insurance covers medical expenses while in France.
- Pharmacies are widely available and can provide advice and over-the-counter medication for minor ailments.
- In case of a medical emergency, call 15 or 112 to request assistance.
- Major hospitals in Nice include Centre Hospitalier Universitaire de Nice and Clinique Saint-George.

Customs and Etiquette

- Greet people with a simple "Bonjour" (good day) or "Bonsoir" (good evening).
- When entering shops or restaurants, it's polite to greet the staff with a "Bonjour" or "Bonsoir."
- It's customary to exchange kisses on both cheeks (la bise) when greeting friends or acquaintances.
- Dress modestly when visiting religious sites, such as churches or cathedrals.
- Learn a few basic French phrases, as locals appreciate the effort, even if they speak English.

Thank you!

As your journey in Nice comes to an end, we hope that this travel guide has been helpful in planning your itinerary and discovering the best attractions, food, and activities that the city has to offer. Whether you visited Nice for its stunning coastline, world-renowned museums, or delicious cuisine, we hope that you have made unforgettable memories that will last a lifetime. Don't forget to take a stroll on the Promenade des Anglais and watch the sunset over the Mediterranean Sea, indulge in some Niçoise cuisine, and immerse yourself in the city's vibrant culture. We wish you a safe journey home and hope to see you again soon in this beautiful city on the French Riviera.

Printed in Great Britain
by Amazon

35845725R00057